CAN I GET SOME HELP OVER HERE?

CYCLE C SERMONS FOR
LENT / EASTER
BASED ON THE GOSPEL TEXTS

R. ROBERT CUENI

CSS PUBLISHING COMPANY, INC.
LIMA, OHIO

CAN I GET SOME HELP OVER HERE?

FIRST EDITION
Copyright © 2015
by CSS Publishing Co., Inc.

Published by CSS Publishing Company, Inc., Lima, Ohio 45807. All rights reserved. No part of this publication may be reproduced in any manner whatsoever without the prior permission of the publisher, except in the case of brief quotations embodied in critical articles and reviews. Inquiries should be addressed to: CSS Publishing Company, Inc., Permissions Department, 5450 N. Dixie Highway, Lima, Ohio 45807.

Library of Congress Cataloging-in-Publication Data

Cueni, R. Robert.
    Can I get some help over here? : Cycle C sermons for Lent/Easter based on the gospel texts / R. Robert Cueni. -- FIRST EDITION.
        pages cm
    ISBN 0-7880-2815-4 (alk. paper)
    1. Lenten sermons. 2. Eastertide--Sermons. 3. Bible. Gospels--Sermons. 4. Sermons, American--21st century. 5. Church year sermons. 6. Common lectionary (1992). Year C. I. Title.

    BV4277.C84   2014
    252'.62--dc23
                                                                    2014037540

For more information about CSS Publishing Company resources, visit our website at www. csspub.com, email us at csr@csspub.com, or call (800) 241-4056.

e-book
ISBN-13: 978-0-7880-2816-8
ISBN-10: 0-7880-2816-2

ISBN-13: 978-0-7880-2815-1
ISBN-10: 0-7880-2815-4   PRINTED IN USA

*To Karl Tillett, beloved son-in-law
and our family's newest American citizen.*

OTHER TITLES WRITTEN BY R. ROBERT CUENI:

WHEN WALLS SHIFT AND THE CEILING COLLAPSES
GOSPEL LESSON, PENTECOST (LAST THIRD), CYCLE C
0-7880-2677-5 / $12.95

SERMONS ON THE GOSPEL READINGS, I, CYCLE C
PENTECOST (LAST THIRD)
0-7880-1968-6 / $38.95

QUESTIONS OF FAITH FOR INQUIRING BELIEVERS
0-7880-1872-8 / $10.95

TENDERS OF THE SACRED FIRE
FIRST LESSON, PENTECOST (FIRST THIRD), CYCLE A
0-7880-0450-6 / $9.95

OTHER TITLES FOR CYCLE C, GOSPEL TEXT
AVAILABLE THROUGH CSS ARE:

GOD WITH SKIN ON
ADVENT/CHRISTMAS/EPIPHANY
BY SUSAN R. ANDREWS

CAN I GET SOME HELP OVER HERE?
LENT/EASTER
BY R. ROBERT CUENI

SPIRIT WORKS
PENTECOST DAY THROUGH PROPER 12
BY ROBERT C. COCHRAN

COUNTING THE COST
PROPER 13 THROUGH PROPER 22
BY GEORGE REED, O.S.L.

ORDINARY GRATITUDE
PROPER 23 THROUGH CHRIST THE KING SUNDAY
BY MOLLY F. JAMES

TABLE OF CONTENTS

PREFACE

This book is a collection of seventeen Cycle C sermons on the gospel readings for the seasons of Lent and Easter. Ten sermons are from John's gospel, six from Luke, and one, a homily for Ash Wednesday, is based on a text from Matthew. Thematically the texts take the reader from the reminder of our human frailty, "You are dust and to dust you shall return," through the agony of Holy Week, to the Hosannas of Easter and Ascension Day.

As I traveled this biblical highway, I kept watching for an overarching theme that might tie the various messages of the texts together. Discerning nothing that expresses a unifying topic any better than the title of one of the sermons, I chose *Can I Get Some Help Over Here?* as the title for the book.

Soon after graduating from seminary forty-some years ago, a mentor challenged me to consider writing for publication as an extension of congregational ministry. With his guidance and encouragement, I agreed to try. What began as a feeble attempt to please a highly respected, older colleague grew into a passionately pursued hobby. Even in retirement, writing continues to be a source of enormous personal satisfaction. I have found that organizing and expressing thoughts to share with those beyond one's congregation a wonderful spiritual and intellectual discipline.

Rather than some species of low-grade self-aggrandizement, this endorsement is intended to encourage the present and next generation of local church ministers to do the same. As one who is coming to the twilight years of active ministry, I can testify that the sweet pain of thinking, writing, rewriting, and rewriting again offers a marvelous way to expend some of life's energy.

7

This thin volume is dedicated to Karl Tillett, our son-in-law. He emigrated to greater Houston from his native Belize in Central America in order to marry our daughter. It has been a great source of delight to watch him respond positively to each new challenge and opportunity presented by a different way of life in a very different country.

What pride I felt when Karl stood with 1,042 people from 126 countries in a moving ceremony of American citizenship. As he held a tiny red, white, and blue flag in his left hand and extended his right hand to take the oath, I thought about how we have always been a nation of immigrants in search of opportunity for a better life. I know that in my family there are stories of previous generations who came to these shores asking, "Can I get some help over here?"

It is nice to know that in spite of the reticence of some, this is still a nation that answers, "Sure. How can we help you?"

Ash Wednesday
Matthew 6:1-6, 16-21

Beware of practicing your piety before others in order to be seen by them; for then you have no reward from your Father in heaven. So whenever you give alms, do not sound a trumpet before you, as the hypocrites do in the synagogues and in the streets, so that they may be praised by others. Truly I tell you, they have received their reward. But when you give alms, do not let your left hand know what your right hand is doing, so that your alms may be done in secret; and your Father who sees in secret will reward you. And whenever you pray, do not be like the hypocrites; for they love to stand and pray in the synagogues and at the street corners, so that they may be seen by others. Truly I tell you, they have received their reward. But whenever you pray, go into your room and shut the door and pray to your Father who is in secret; and your Father who sees in secret will reward you.... And whenever you fast, do not look dismal, like the hypocrites, for they disfigure their faces so as to show others that they are fasting. Truly I tell you, they have received their reward. But when you fast, put oil on your head and wash your face, so that your fasting may be seen not by others but by your Father who is in secret; and your Father who sees in secret will reward you. Do not store up for yourselves treasures on earth, where moth and rust consume and where thieves break in and steal; but store up for yourselves treasures in heaven, where neither moth nor rust consumes and where thieves do not break in and steal. For where your treasure is, there your heart will be also.

GOOD-BYE MARDI GRAS, HELLO LENT

Lent, the season of preparation for Easter, begins today. Traditionally, Lent is marked by prayer, fasting, self-reflection, and repentance. Lent is sufficiently serious that some Christian calendars have installed a season to prepare for it. It is called Mardi Gras. Whereas Lent projects a somber, almost lugubrious mood with a theme of denial and self-discipline, Mardi Gras is just the opposite. It is a time for parades, parties, and dancing in the streets.

The celebration called Mardi Gras is, of course, big in New Orleans, but I understand it is even bigger in Rio de Janeiro. The Brazilians call their festival Rio Carnival. Most businesses in the city close for a full week. Workers are given a holiday to attend this 24-hour per day colorful gala in the city streets. Every year five million people, including 400,000 foreign visitors, prepare for Lent by attending Rio's biggest party.

I have never experienced Mardi Gras or Rio Carnival. I am considering putting them on my bucket list. Unfortunately, that will have to wait for another year. The parties ended yesterday. The Irish poet, Thomas Moore captures the feeling.

I feel like one
Who treads alone
Some banquet-hall deserted,
Whose lights are fled,

11

Whose garlands dead,
And all but he departed.[1]

Today begins Lent. We set aside the colorful bead neck-laces of Mardi Gras and receive the ashen mark of the cross. We replace the samba rhythms of Rio and the jazz beat of New Orleans' Dirty Dozen Brass Band with reminders of our finitude and the gospel call: "You are dust and to dust you shall return" (Genesis 3:19); "repent, and believe the good news" (Mark 1:15).

The lectionary gospel reading for the day comes from the heart of the Sermon on the Mount. In this passage Jesus lays out a standard of behavior for three acts of piety: alms-giving, prayer, and fasting. Succinctly stated, the message is that when followers of Jesus Christ engage in these faith practices, we should do so secretly, without a trace of phoni-ness and without any expectation of external reward. Our acts of devotion in giving, praying, and fasting are to rise out of our commitment to Christ. These acts of piety are to be their own reward.

Matthew 6 begins, "Beware of practicing your piety be-fore others in order to be seen by them; for then you have no reward from your Father in heaven. So whenever you give alms, do not sound a trumpet before you" (vv. 1-2).

In his book, *Unwinding America*, George Parker dis-cusses Sam Walton, a man of humble beginnings who be-came one of the richest men in America. He says of Walton that he was "cautious about money." Even after he became a billionaire, he would stop to pick up a nickel on the side-walk. He still got a five-dollar haircut in downtown Benton-ville and he still didn't leave a tip. To quote Parker, "He and his company gave almost nothing to charity. But every year each Walmart store would hand out a thousand-dollar col-lege scholarship to a local high school senior, and somehow that bought better publicity than generous corporate philan-thropy."[2]

Maximizing the impact of every dollar spent can be defended as a good business practice. On the other hand, giving for the purpose of maximizing publicity runs contrary to the biblical standard.

Admittedly, an accusation can be made that the church talks too much about money. There is truth in that, but there is also a reason for it. Few things in American life are more important to us than money and the things it will buy. Money is a driving force in our politics, our governance, our family life, and our personal lives. Money is even a driving force in the business life of the church. Despite what some claim, however, it is not true that "all the church wants is our money." Actually, our faith expects a great deal more than our money.

A minister friend tells the story of an evangelism call he made on man who had been attending church. The minister stopped one Saturday morning to ask if this fellow was ready to confess his faith in the lordship of Jesus Christ. When the minister arrived at the house, the man was working in his lawn. As the minister got out of his car, the man good naturedly tossed his wallet to him. "I bet you came to ask me for money. Well there it is. Take it." The minister returned the wallet and told the man, "I didn't come for your money. I came for your life."

Christ gave his life for us. Everything we are and everything we have is a gift of God. When you give, give out of thanksgiving for the gift of life. "Do not sound a trumpet before you as the hypocrites do." This is the gospel and the message is clear: "You are dust and to dust you shall return; repent, and believe the gospel."

The word translated there as "hypocrite" is the Greek word for "actor." An actor is one who puts on a costume and pretends to be something or someone he or she is not. The directive not to be a hypocrite is to say, "Don't practice your faith as though you are playing a role in a movie. Don't be the person you think will impress others. Be the person God calls you to be."

Jesus uses the same term a few verses later. "And whenever you pray, do not be like the hypocrites; for they love to stand and pray in the synagogues and at the street corners, so that they might be seen by others. Truly I tell you, they have received their reward" (v. 5).

A friend named Jim told me it happened years ago. He and his wife were newly engaged. Some of her relatives invited them to a very nice restaurant for dinner. Before that gathering, his soon-to-be wife warned him that this particular branch of her clan was very pious. She explained, "Alcohol is never served, so don't order a drink. They will use a great deal of religious language — even when religion is not the topic of conversation. You might be quizzed about your church attendance. Please just smile, nod, and politely answer their questions. Please don't start a religious debate with them. And whatever you do, don't sit down at the table until Uncle Edgar says the prayer. It is just their way of doing things."

Jim said, "I thought I was ready, but the experience was much worse than I anticipated. The hostess led us to a big table in the middle of the restaurant. There must have been a dozen of us. We all stood behind our chairs, joined hands, and waited while Uncle Edgar prayed in a voice loud enough for everyone in the building to hear and long enough for everyone to turn their attention toward our table." Jim concluded by saying, "If I had been wearing a long prayer shawl with dangling tassels, I could not have felt more like one of those Pharisees in the Bible."

To paraphrase the words of our Lord, "Don't stand and pray in a loud voice at the street corner or around the table at the restaurant. When you pray in order to get the attention of others, you have already received your reward." That is the message of our faith. That is the gospel and the message is clear: "You are dust and to dust you shall return; repent, and believe the gospel."

After dealing with faithful ways to pray and to give alms, Jesus turns his attention to a third act of piety: fasting. "And whenever you fast, do not look dismal, like the hypocrites, for they disfigure their faces so as to show others they are fasting" (v. 16). When you fast don't make a big deal out of it; don't twist your face as if you have just eaten a sour pickle; don't walk up to a stranger in the street and say "Did I tell you I am fasting? That is why God thinks I am very special."

Although fasting for religious purposes is done today, many of us are more familiar with the practice as preparation for a blood test at the doctor's office. Obviously, that was not its significance in the biblical era. Religiously, fasting was and is a means to come closer to God. The idea is that by denying oneself food, one's attention can be better focused on matters of the faith. Fasting promotes self-denial as a religious discipline.

Unfortunately, self-denial of any sort is not high on our list of priorities. We live in a time more attuned to self-indulgence than self-denial. In fact, we tend not to want to deny ourselves much of anything. Yet our faith teaches there is spiritual value in self-denial. That is the reason behind the tradition of "giving up something for Lent." It is the practice of self-denial. Give up something for Lent. A little self-denial is good for you.

A common fasting practice of the biblical era was to throw ashes over your head and let them drift down on your face as part of the fast. Apparently some people liked to walk around the streets that way so that they could claim a little attention from others. "Hey, look at me, I am fasting. I am being religious." Jesus offered a corrective, "And whenever you fast, do not look dismal, like the hypocrites... but when you fast, put oil on your head and wash your face." The reward of self-denial is a closer relationship to God, not the admiration of others.

Charitable giving, prayer, and self-denial are acts of piety that bring us closer to God. Engage in them without a trace of phoniness and without any expectation of external reward. This is the gospel and the message is clear: "You are dust and to dust you shall return; repent, and believe the gospel."

We share today the ancient practice of imposing ashes in the shape of the cross. The usual tradition is not to remove the ashes. Instead let the ashes be worn off by the passing of time. If you are headed straight home, that is a tradition to be practiced. If, however, you are headed to a restaurant or plan to pick up a few things at the grocery, you might want to remove the ashes. Strangers might think you didn't hear the sermon today. They might think you are showing off.

---

1. Thomas Moore (1779-1852) "Oft in the Stilly Night" a part of the second stanza from *National Airs*, c. 1822, p. 7.

2. George Parker, *The Unwinding: An Inner History of the New America* (New York: Farrar, Straus & Giroux, 2013), pp. 100-102.

Lent 1
Luke 4:1-13

Jesus, full of the Holy Spirit, returned from the Jordan and was led by the Spirit in the wilderness, where for forty days he was tempted by the devil. He ate nothing at all during those days, and when they were over, he was famished. The devil said to him, "If you are the Son of God, command this stone to become a loaf of bread." Jesus answered him, "It is written, 'One does not live by bread alone.' " Then the devil led him up and showed him in an instant all the kingdoms of the world. And the devil said to him, "To you I will give their glory and all this authority; for it has been given over to me, and I give it to anyone I please. If you, then, will worship me, it will all be yours." Jesus answered him, "It is written, 'Worship the Lord your God, and serve only him.' " Then the devil took him to Jerusalem, and placed him on the pinnacle of the temple, saying to him, "If you are the Son of God, throw yourself down from here, for it is written, 'He will command his angels concerning you, to protect you,' and 'On their hands they will bear you up, so that you will not dash your foot against a stone.' " Jesus answered him, "It is said, 'Do not put the Lord your God to the test.' " When the devil had finished every test, he departed from him until an opportune time.

WHAT TO GIVE UP
FOR LENT

The Faithful Followers Sunday School class at the Church of What's Happening Now was discussing the upcoming season of Lent. The congregation had never had such a discussion. This congregation prided itself on their core value of relevance. Adhering to ancient seasons such as Advent and Lent simply did not rise to that standard. Their church calendar had a softball schedule but no mention of Lent.

Their new pastor, however, had suggested the congregation might find the rhythm of a traditional church calendar spiritually enriching. He said they might even find it relevant. The Faithful Followers Sunday School class was not convinced but wanted to be supportive of their new leader and decided to give it a try.

In the past few weeks, they had learned Lent is to be a time of preparation for Easter; a time of enhanced participation in worship, Bible study, prayer, and wrestling with the deeper questions of faith; a time to ready oneself to better experience the passion, death, and resurrection of Jesus the Christ. Integral to spiritual preparation for Easter is to spend some time thinking about the obstacles faced daily that keep Christians from living the lives of faithful followers. Lenten self-reflection was never to be an end unto itself. Obstacles and temptations were not only to be identified, they were to be corrected.

Joyce, often the one to offer insightful observations, ventured a comment. "That must be where the idea of giving up something for Lent originated. We are to identify obstacles and temptation in our lives that have become stumbling blocks in our Christian walk. Then we are to eliminate them or, at the very least, refrain from them during Lent."

Bill, always ready to demonstrate his technological savvy, chimed in. "Did you know there are actually websites that make suggestions for what to give up during Lent? I wrote down some ideas. Give up favorite foods like cake, ice cream, pizza, fried chicken, soft drinks, or coffee. Curtail the time spent on favorite activities like television, golf, shopping, computer use, Facebook, Twitter, and endless back and forth texting with friends. There were even suggestions about eliminating a bad habit, such as excessive alcohol use, smoking, lying, gossip, road rage, procrastination, or foul language."

John interrupted Bill before he finished his list. "Give up road rage for Lent? For me, that would be relevant. I commute an hour to work and an hour home every day. Traffic is always heavy. Sometimes the freeway resembles a long, narrow parking lot. I spend too much of the commute screaming at bad drivers, pounding the steering wheel when someone changes lanes without signaling, and expressing my displeasure with obscene gestures. My rage carries into the office in the morning and into my home in the evening. I need to stop it. I am going to work on giving up anger for Lent."

Other Faithful Followers took the conversation in different directions. Susie, a former college English major and stay-at-home mother of an infant, interjected: "I keep the television on during the day. I am starting to realize cable news has become a raging river of idle chatter and I am drowning in it. The 24/7 news stations chew on the same events and issues for hour after hour, day after day. If there is a tragedy

20

anywhere in the country that becomes fresh fodder for constant chatter. How many interviews do they need with people who have just lost their home in a tornado? Those people feel terrible. Why keep asking? One cable network spent hours every day for months talking about a murder trial. A young woman was charged with killing her boyfriend. If she was found guilty that young woman could be sentenced to death. Yet the lives of that boyfriend and girlfriend were discussed as if the story was a soap opera with consequences no more serious than losing the race on a reality show. I have become too involved in listening to that stuff. Emotionally, that constant negative chatter drags me down. I am going to turn it off for Lent."

Still others in the class talked about excessive participation on social media. One admitted spending so many hours each day communicating with friends on Facebook that she was neglecting face-to-face communication with loved ones at home. Another in the class concurred, "I think my wife, my children, and I need a serious sit down discussion about giving up social media for Lent." By the end of Sunday school, the Faithful Followers came to understand that giving up something for Lent can be far more relevant than first assumed.

With that as background, let us turn our attention to the gospel reading for today from Luke 4:1-13. Here we are told that immediately after baptism by John, Jesus went alone to a desolate place in the wilderness. Apparently, he went with hopes of having quiet time to fast, to pray, and to seek the presence of God before he began his ministry. Unfortunately, his spiritual retreat was anything but quiet. Luke tells us the devil showed up with a pocketful of temptations. Jesus had to resist these enticements lest they undermine and destroy his ministry.

Although they usually appear to us in modified formats, we still face these temptations. They still ensnare the vulnerable. They still have the power to undermine and destroy. Each of us needs to examine our life carefully to see if there is something in this biblical narrative we might need to give up for Lent.

Luke tells us the first thing the devil did was to try to take advantage of Jesus' physical needs. The master had been fasting. More than a little hungry, he was so famished it was difficult to think of anything else. The devil picked up a stone and held it in his hand. The evil one smiled and suggested that if Jesus was really the Son of God, he should turn the stone into bread. That bread would satisfy his most immediate physical need — his hunger. Jesus resisted by telling the tempter that we cannot live by bread alone.

Turning stone to bread doesn't seem much of a temptation. In fact, it can be argued that this is a possibility to pursue; not a temptation to avoid. Bread is a generic term for food and a euphemism for money and all it will buy. If we could turn stones to bread, we could vanquish famine and lift the desperately poor out of poverty. In that sense, turning stones to bread would be a good thing.

Yes, it would, but Jesus resisted the opportunity. He understood that the abundant life requires more than bread as food and money. Satisfying physical needs and material wants does not guarantee happiness. Even an overabundance of bread as food and money will not satisfy the underlying existential hunger for meaning and purpose. We need bread but the abundant life does not come by bread alone.

Where are you on this issue? Do you harbor any lingering notion that if you just had a little more money or just acquired a few more possessions you could really be happy? If so, you might want to think about giving up that idea for

Lent. You might want to commit yourself to pray and study on why people do not live by bread alone.

After his initial failure, the devil tried a new approach. In the twinkling of an eye, the devil took Jesus to a place where all the kingdoms and empires were brought into view. Jesus was told that if he would worship the devil, he could rule the world "Think of that Jesus, for a little bowing and scraping, you can be CEO and Chairman of the Board for everything."

To literally rule the world is not something most of us find particularly tempting. On the other hand, most of us would appreciate having a little more control of our little corner our world. "It would be wonderful if I could get my significant other to do what I want, when I want, and in the manner I want. If only I could make all the decisions for my children or my parents. If only I could control my employees, my boss, or my students."

It is tempting to want to have control. Unfortunately, it is never really possible. We can make an argument that if others would do as we tell them, their lives would improve significantly. Unfortunately, others harbor this notion that they still want to make their own decisions. No matter how hard we plan, unexpected and unwanted things occur. We try to avoid it, but we still fail from time to time. We live in a world where we never really have total control. The temptation is dangled in front of us, but it can never be.

Coming to terms with the reality that you are not in charge is actually very liberating. If they ever organize a 12-step program called "Control Freaks Anonymous," the guiding principle will be: "The best day of your life comes when you admit that you cannot take credit for keeping the stars spangled in the heavens and you need not take responsibility for keeping the earth turning on its axis."

Jesus saw the danger of trying to rule the empires and kingdoms of the world. Rather than being in control, Jesus understood that victorious living comes by learning to let go and trust God. How are you doing with issues of control? Is that something you need to consider giving up for Lent?

Not one to give up easily, the evil one tried one more thing. He took Jesus to the tallest pinnacle of the temple in Jerusalem. He told Jesus that he could dive off that spire and not get hurt. If he was really the messiah, God would send angels to rescue him before he splattered in the courtyard. Jesus resisted the temptation by telling the devil: "Do not put the Lord your God to the test."

As with the others, this temptation doesn't seem particularly relevant for us. Certainly a normal, mentally healthy person is not likely to feel tempted to take a nose dive off a high building just to test whether or not God will send a choir of angels to the rescue. There must be some psychiatric diagnosis for that.

On the other hand, we are tempted to test God. Keep in mind that our relationship to God is not dissimilar to a small but ornery child's relationship to a loving, patient parent. "Jimmy, how many times do I have to tell you not to stand on the furniture?" "If you kids don't stop fighting I am going to stop this car. I get so tired of your misbehaving."

Children test parents and parents grow so weary of it. In that same way, as God's children, we test the limits and God must get so tired of it. We claim Christ as the Prince of Peace, yet too often over the centuries we have gone to war under the banner of Christ. When we do that, we test God. God must weary of it.

In Christ we are called to care for the most vulnerable. Certainly children are vulnerable. Yet we have read of too many of those called to be leaders of Christ's church who have molested children rather than protected them. God must so weary of the failings of people who call themselves Christians. We test God.

Our faith teaches that we are to love our enemy and do good to those who hate us. We try but Jesus never faced an enemy like ours. Even when we strive to love our enemy, their hate for us remains. We have seen how we can welcome our enemy into this nation, feed them, clothe them, provide for them a place to live and money to go to college. As an expression of their thanks they might even explode bombs at the finish line of the Boston Marathon. Our expressions of love only deepened their hate for us. We do test God, but God also tests us.

What should we give up for Lent? On the one hand that question is simple to answer. Give up something that keeps you from being the person God calls you to be. On the other hand, deciding precisely what that might be and how to give it up can require an enormous amount of study, prayer, and deep spiritual reflections. Of course, those are the practices at the heart of the Lenten preparation for Easter.

May God bless you in your wrestling with the question of what to give up for Lent.

Lent 2
Luke 13:31-35

At that very hour some Pharisees came and said to him, "Get away from here, for Herod wants to kill you." He said to them, "Go and tell that fox for me, 'Listen, I am casting out demons and performing cures today and tomorrow, and on the third day I finish my work. Yet today, tomorrow, and the next day I must be on my way, because it is impossible for a prophet to be killed outside of Jerusalem.' Jerusalem, Jerusalem, the city that kills the prophets and stones those who are sent to it! How often have I desired to gather your children together as a hen gathers her brood under her wings, and you were not willing! See, your house is left to you. And I tell you, you will not see me until the time comes when you say, 'Blessed is the one who comes in the name of the Lord.'"

IT IS ALWAYS
THE THIRD DAY

We know the story well. Jesus was journeying toward Jerusalem. When he arrived in the capital city, he would be welcomed with a great parade. The crowd along the main street would cheer, "Blessed is the one who comes in the name of the Lord" (Matthew 13:35). A few days after that, the crowd would turn on Jesus. He would face a trial, crucifixion, death, and burial. Then, on the third day, Christ would be raised from the dead. On the third day, there would be new life. As Amos Wilder, a distinguished Harvard New Testament scholar wrote:

Retell, renew the event
In these planetary years,
For we were there and He is here;
It is always the third day.[1]

Treasure that assurance in the front of your mind. It is always the third day. As Jesus and the apostles walked toward Jerusalem, the group stopped now and again for Jesus to preach the gospel, heal the sick, and cast out demons. By necessity, these stops were brief because Jesus had a rendezvous with destiny in Jerusalem. In a quiet moment at one of these stops, a group of Pharisees alerted Jesus to impending danger. "Get away from here, for (King) Herod wants to kill you" (v. 31).

Luke's gospel does not mention the Pharisees' motivation. It may have been heartfelt. The Pharisees may have heard of a plot against Jesus and wanted to warn him. On the other hand, their motive may have been more sinister. Maybe they were threatened by Jesus and wanted to move him along. "Get away from here for Herod wants to kill you."

As background information, understand there was more than one king named Herod. At the time of Jesus' birth, Herod the Great was king. When the Magi stopped to ask for directions so they could visit the baby boy born "king of the Jews," Herod the Great ordered the deaths of all baby boys under the age of two. Infant genocide was this Herod's method of getting rid of a perceived rival. Herod the Great was an especially vicious fellow.

His grandson, Herod Agrippa was known for extravagant spending on himself, being excessively greedy, taking bribes, and colluding with the Romans. Agrippa became king by falsely accusing his uncle of being disloyal to Caligula, the Roman emperor. Like his grandfather, Herod Agrippa was not a nice person.

Agrippa's uncle, King Herod Antipas was ruler during the ministry of Jesus. Antipas was the Herod who had John the Baptist arrested and beheaded. He was also instrumental in the trial of Jesus. As with his father and nephew, Herod Antipas had a bad reputation. (Evil seemed to run in this family.)

When the Pharisees told Jesus, "Get away from here, Herod wants to kill you," they might have been literally referring to Herod Antipas. On the other hand, they may have been using the name as shorthand for the usual bad behavior of all the local rulers. Whatever their motivation and to whomever the Pharisees referred, Jesus responded to their warning to get out of town by saying, "Go tell that fox."

Today, to call someone a "fox" is to say something positive. "Wow! That is one foxy lady" or "He's a fox." That is not true here. Almost always, the Bible portrays the fox in a negative light. The reason is obvious. A fox is physically beautiful, but it is a vicious, sneaky, tricky, unrelenting predator. The fox leaves a trail of destruction and death in its wake.

To paraphrase Jesus' response to the Pharisees' warning, "Go tell that vicious, predatory old fox that I am occupied with other matters today and tomorrow, but remember this, the third day will come." No matter how threatening the world might be today and tomorrow, life's cruel ways will not last. Resurrection is coming. New life comes on the third day and it is always the third day.

Within this short discourse is also a magnificent simile of Jesus' love, not only for the residents of Jerusalem, but a simile of God's love for all people. "How often I have desired to gather your children together as a hen gathers her brood under her wings."

Many, if not most of us have no firsthand experience of the behavior Jesus described. Our personal experience with chickens is limited to freshly packaged at the grocery store or cooked and ready to eat from the Colonel at KFC. Jesus' audience, however, knew chicken behavior. For thousands of years, they were raised in the backyard. People lived with chickens. They watched them every day. They had watched hens react to impending threat. For instance, when a fox first came into view, the hen started to bring her chicks under the shelter of her wings. If the fox got too close, the hen launched an attack against the predator. The hen was willing to sacrifice her life for her brood. Jesus tells us that God's love for us is like that. "There have been so many times that I wanted to gather the children of God together as a hen gathers her brood under her wings."

On the one hand, that is a warm and wonderful simile. We should not, however, misunderstand. The hen cannot guarantee her brood an under-wing safe haven from misfortune. In fact, the mother hen rarely wins a battle with the fox. She is selfless in her devotion to her little ones but she is no match for the long claws and sharp teeth of the predator. Unless there is some other intervention, the fox will likely kill and eat the hen. Then, if it fits his fancy, the fox will kill and eat the chicks as well.

Frankly, this is a fitting description for the reality of the world in which we live. God's love for us is unconditional. We can and will be redeemed by the sacrificial love of God in Christ Jesus. God's love does not, however, protect us from all the threats and ravages of this world. There are some really miserable things that can and do happen. Alfred Lord Tennyson wrote of this harsh reality of the human condition by saying:

> *Who trusted God was love indeed*
> *And love (is) Creation's final law*
> *Tho' Nature, red in tooth and claw*
> *With ravine, shriek'd against his creed* [2]

It was in the middle of a cold northern Michigan winter. The inland lakes had been frozen solid for weeks. There were two couples in their early thirties. Each had two children less than ten years of age. Both families were highly regarded in the community. That 56 mile snowmobile safari around Lake Charlevoix's shoreline seemed a wonderful idea. The fathers had checked their route the previous week. The ice was several feet thick. It was safe. They started the adventure early Saturday morning. The parents rode the snowmobiles with the kids towed behind on sleds. The plan was to stop in the little town of East Jordan for breakfast. They were driving on the ice into the rising sun and didn't see that a tributary, the Jordan River had opened a channel in the ice.

The snowmobiles, sleds, and all eight travelers went into the cold, open water. With the added burdens of machinery and heavy, wet winter clothing, both parents in one family and a small child in the other family drowned.

What a terrible tragedy! Two families were ripped asunder because a stream beneath the ice had intersected with the warm rays of the winter's sun. To paraphrase Tennyson, God's love may be the final law, but we live in a world where nature is red in tooth and claw.

We see this all around us. A tornado hits a neighborhood and destroys a hundred homes. A hurricane wipes out a shoreline and costs millions to repair. A drought destroys crops and kills trees. A flood floats one home down the river and fills the others with two feet of stinking mud. Nature is red in tooth and claw. We are always vulnerable to the fox.

Of course, not all the threats come from nature. In T.S. Eliot's play *The Cocktail Party*,[3] one of the characters is Celia Coplestone. An accomplished person, Celia longs for happiness and meaning in her life. She has tried the social attractions: theatre, receptions, cocktail parties, even an affair with Edward, another character in the play. Cecilia has tried it all, yet something is missing. She goes to a psychiatrist. In time, Celia has an insight. The source of her existential anxiety lies not in the world around her, but as T.S. Eliot causes her to say, "There is something wrong with me."

Cecilia came to realize that she is the fox in her own life. Human beings are threatened and harmed, not only by outside forces, but by our own decisions. It is another of the givens of the human condition. In the midst of trying to convince Brutus to join the conspiracy against Julius Caesar, Shakespeare caused Cassius to make the same point, "The fault, dear Brutus, is not in our stars but in ourselves."[4]

In her spiritual autobiography, *Traveling Mercies*,[5] the popular writer, Ann Lamott described how as a child, she

33

had a friend whose father was in prison and whose mother was an alcoholic. Ann says that even though that friend's family life was dysfunctional, she preferred spending her time there. Ann explained that there was consistency in that house. Her friend's father was always in prison and her mother was always drunk. At Ann Lamott's house, one never knew what was going to happen next. By the time she was in her early thirties, Ann had descended into a life of drug addiction, alcohol abuse, and promiscuity.

Ann Lamott knew what Cecilia Coplestone meant when she said, "There is something wrong with me." Yet, Ann also listened for the hope in the next line T.S. Eliot gave Cecilia, "There is something wrong with me *that could be put right*." Whatever is wrong with us can be put right. That is the hope.

Ann's life was put right when she came to know Jesus Christ and the power of his resurrection. She said that her conversion took place, not as an instantaneous leap of faith, but as a series of staggers from what seemed like one safe place to another.

Along the way, there was a minister who listened — really listened. There was a little church in the neighborhood where she heard the music from the street long before she found the courage to enter. Then there came a certain night in the midst of a medical emergency. She was falling down drunk. It was late at night. She was at home alone. She felt someone with her in the dark. She claimed she just knew beyond all doubt that it was the presence of Jesus. A week later she stopped resisting. "I shouted, '[expletive deleted] I quit. You can come in now.' "

Ann's life was changed. She was set on the right path by the power of the presence of God encountered in the course of an ordinary day; an ordinary day that proved to be one of those third day encounters.

You never know just when you or someone you know will say, "There is something wrong with me, but I believe it can be set right." Indeed it can, but it takes one of those third day encounters. Fortunately, as Amos Wilder put it:

Retell, renew the event
In these planetary years,
For we were there and (God) is here:
It is always the third day.[6]

Thanks be to God. Amen and Amen.

———————

1. From the website joyfulpapist.wordpress.com/2010/04/09/it-is-always-the-third-day/

2. Alfred Lord Tennyson, Canto 56, *In Memoriam A.H.H.*, 1850.

3. T.S. Eliot, *The Cocktail Party* (New York: Harcourt Brace, 1950).

4. William Shakespeare, *Julius Caesar*, Act 1, Scene 2, p. 6.

5. Ann Lamott, *Traveling Mercies: Some Thoughts on Faith* (New York: Pantheon Books, 1999).

6. From the website joyfulpapist.wordpress.com/2010/04/09/it-is-always-the-third-day/

Lent 3
Luke 13:1-9

At that very time there were some present who told him about the Galileans whose blood Pilate had mingled with their sacrifices. He asked them, "Do you think that because these Galileans suffered in this way they were worse sinners than all other Galileans? No, I tell you; but unless you repent, you will all perish as they did. Or those eighteen who were killed when the tower of Siloam fell on them — do you think that they were worse offenders than all the others living in Jerusalem? No, I tell you; but unless you repent, you will all perish just as they did." Then he told this parable: "A man had a fig tree planted in his vineyard; and he came looking for fruit on it and found none. So he said to the gardener, 'See here! For three years I have come looking for fruit on this fig tree, and still I find none. Cut it down! Why should it be wasting the soil?' He replied, 'Sir, let it alone for one more year, until I dig around it and put manure on it. If it bears fruit next year, well and good; but if not, you can cut it down.'"

WHAT TO DO
WITH HUMAN FAILING

As with most employment, pastoral ministry has occupational hazards. I don't want to overstate the case. Ministry is not potentially lethal as it is for police, firefighters, or combat infantry. By comparison, ministry's hazards are irritations, mere inconveniences.

For instance, simply being a minister is an obstacle to making new friends. Let us say you are the new pastor in town. Probably by accident, you receive an invitation to a rip-roaring Neighborhood Association New Year's Eve party. At that gathering, if you want to make new friends, don't open conversations by mentioning your occupation. Wild party attenders tend to be uncomfortable around unfamiliar clergy. Announcing a pastoral vocation at 10:00 p.m. may mean that by 10:30, you are standing alone in a dark corner. There are exceptions, of course. Undertakers are frequently paired with clergy on New Year's Eve. Being a minister changes the dynamic of turning strangers into friends.

Commercial airline travel can also be an occupational hazard. At 30,000 feet, strangers often want to wax eloquently to a newly met minister about their personally constructed, yet incredibly faulty theological conclusions. "Well, I never go to church, but I believe Christianity requires only that you be a nice person, not steal anything of great value, and never intentionally kill anyone. That pretty well says it all. Don't you agree, Reverend?"

The temptation is to answer, "Yes, that certainly summarizes Christianity as well as 'Twinkle, twinkle little star' summarizes astrophysics." That, I have learned by experience, is best left unsaid. Theologically uninformed airline passengers consider themselves entitled to pontificate on their religious views. It matters not how simplistic, erroneous, or even silly those views may be. Ministers spend years doing in-depth Bible study, learning the history and teachings of the church, and honing the skills needed for constructive theology and critical thinking. Yet attempting to negotiate a meaningful conversation with the theologically uninformed or misinformed is generally a waste of time.

I have learned the best way to deal with this occupational hazard is to apply what we in the trade call an *S&N* — Smile and Nod knowingly. Then instead of responding, "That is the dumbest comment I have ever heard," try to look interested and say, "I don't think I have ever heard it said quite that way before."

I mention this simply as background for today's gospel lesson. Jesus was embroiled in a difficult conversation on a very complex issue. The subject was causality. Why do certain things happen? It can and often is argued that there is a reason for everything. If that is true, how does one discern the reason? What is the cause/effect relationship? Was that just an accident, a serendipitous confluence of human behavior with the laws of nature or did God cause it to happen? And if God caused it, why did God do that?

Without providing a comprehensive understanding, today's gospel lesson touches on a tiny slice of causality. The topic is introduced in Luke 12:54-56. To paraphrase, Jesus said to the crowd, "Everyone knows the causes of weather. When dark clouds come from the Mediterranean Sea in the west, you know rain will likely follow. Dark clouds cause rain. When a strong breeze blows from the south, you know it is going to be hot that day. Wind from the south causes a scorching day. You know about weather. Why don't you understand what causes things to happen to people?"

In my humble opinion, the best answer to Jesus' question is that "we know how the weather works because it is easy to understand weather. It doesn't take a Ph.D. in meteorology to figure out that when dark clouds appear, rain is likely. That is very different from discerning why the righteous suffer, why the wicked prosper, why bad things happen to good people, or why good people do bad things."

Without acknowledging the complex and mysterious nature of human causalities, in the first verses of Luke 13, people in Jesus' audience try their hand at naming the cause of a recent event. As best we can piece the incident together, a group of Galileans had been on a religious pilgrimage to Jerusalem. At the great temple, these folks participated in the regular ritual animal sacrifices. Somehow they got caught crosswise with Pontius Pilate. The Roman governor dispatched a squad of soldiers to slaughter the pilgrims. As Luke's gospel puts it, "At that time there were some present (in the crowd) who told him (Jesus) about the Galileans whose blood Pilate had mingled with their sacrifices" (v. 1).

That event, of course, would have made front page headlines in the Galilean Daily News: "Pontius Pilate Slaughters Ten Galileans." Everybody in town would have been talking about it. People would have wanted to know how and why it happened. It is logical to conclude that the chatter would have been rampant. Luke does not say specifically, but apparently one of the theories floating around Galilee was that the victims were responsible for their own deaths: "They must have all been evil people. God used the Romans to punish them for their sins."

When Jesus heard this gossipy explanation he said to the crowd,

Do you (really) think that because these Galileans suf-
fered in this way they were worse sinners than all other
Galileans? No, I tell you; but unless you repent, you will
all perish as they did. Or those eighteen who were killed
when the tower of Siloam fell on them — do you think they
were worse offenders than all the others living in Jeru-
salem? No, I tell you; but unless you repent, you will all
perish just as they did.
(vv. 1-5)

Obviously, Jesus was not impressed by the argument that the best way to identify sinners was to see who got killed by a falling tower or by Pontius Pilate. (To paraphrase) "No, I tell you," Jesus said, "there is no cause/effect relationship between being one of the worst sinners in Galilee and having your blood mingled with the blood of sacrificed animals, and you cannot explain the deaths of eighteen killed when the Tower of Siloam collapsed by concluding those folks were worse offenders than all the others living in Jerusalem. God does not work that way and there is no law of the natural world that holds bad folks can always be identified by the terrible things that happen to them. It just does not work that way."

Even twenty centuries later we hear echoes of this erroneous thinking. One morning a few years ago at Connecticut's Sandy Hook Elementary School, a deeply disturbed young man used three semi-automatic firearms to murder twenty small children and six adults. Before the outrage and grief could be fully exhausted, the internet crackled with comments about how parents and school officials were really the ones at fault. They had just not adequately protected the school or the children. A few even commented that they believed that if the teachers had been armed, this would not have happened.

No, I tell you. It was not the fault of those tourists in Jerusalem that they were killed by Roman soldiers and it was not the school or the parents who were responsible for the deaths at Sandy Hook Elementary School. That is simply not the way it works.

On September 11, 2001, commercial airliners were intentionally crashed into the twin towers of the World Trade Center in New York City. It was part of a wider coordinated attack that day by al-Qaeda, an Islamic international terrorist network. When the tower at Siloam fell eighteen people were killed. When the towers at the World Trade Center collapsed nearly 3,000 people died. The victims were as diverse as millionaire investment bankers on the middle floors, minimum wage restaurant workers on the top floor, and first responding firefighters in the lobby. All of them were there just to do their jobs.

Two days later, on September 13, two television evangelists broadcast their analysis to the nation. They were essentially in agreement when one said, "God has lifted the curtain and has allowed the enemies of America to give us what we probably deserve."[1] Then the two made a list of incidents, people, causes, and organizations that they were certain had "made God mad" and therefore had to share the blame for the attack.

No, I tell you, it doesn't work that way. It was wrong to conclude that a tower falling in Siloam had something to do with God's punishment for sinfulness. It is equality wrong to conclude that a falling tower in lower Manhattan had something to do with God's punishment for sinfulness. God does not work that way.

To say that, of course, begs the question, "If not by dropping a tower on them, how does God deal with sinful people?" That issue is important for every one of us. After all, we are all included in the category of sinful people. As

43

Paul put it, "For there is no distinction, since all have sinned and fall short of the glory of God" (Romans 3:22b-23). The inquiring mind should want to know how God deals with our having sinned and have fallen short of God's glory. Jesus anticipated that turn in the conversation so he told the parable of the barren fig tree:

> *A man had a fig tree planted in his vineyard; and he came looking for fruit on it and found none. So he said to the gardener, "See here! For three years I have come looking for fruit on this fig tree, and still I find none. Cut it down! Why should it be wasting the soil?" He replied, "Sir, let it alone for one more year, until I dig around it and put manure on it. If it bears fruit next year, well and good; but if not, you can cut it down."*
> (Luke 13:6-9)

Notice what is happening in this story. A backyard fig tree has yet to produce figs. The owner suggests giving up and cutting the tree down. The gardener suggests another way. Give it more time and a little tender loving care. Loosen the soil and apply some fertilizer. Give it another year. If it still doesn't produce figs, the option of cutting it down will still be available.

Rather than offering a benign smile and nod and moving to the next question, Jesus turned the focus, content, and tone of this conversation upside down and inside out. This ceased being a chat about whether or not total strangers had been killed as punishment for their sinfulness. Now it was a conversation about how God dealt with all sinners — including and, perhaps especially, the sinners in his audience.

What Jesus said is that rather than dropping towers on those who have failed to live up to God's standards, we are given another chance. In response to our miserable failings, God offers radical grace. We experience the grace as a loos-

44

ening of the hard-packed soil around our hearts. God deals with us sinners, not by dropping a tower on us, but by giving us a big dose of unconditional love. This is radical grace as another chance, a new opportunity. The Franciscan priest, Richard Rohr put it so well: "Most of us were taught that God would love us if and when we change. In fact, God loves you so that you can change. What empowers change... is the experience of love. It is that inherent experience of love that becomes the engine of change."[2]

The tone of this conversation is now different. No longer does it feel as though dark stormy clouds of judgment are gathering. No longer is there a hot wind of hades blowing. Now there seems to be a cool gentle breeze and a bright blue sky. That is the difference Jesus makes. As Richard Rohr put it, "The true gospel is always fresh air and breathing room."

And for that radical grace of another change, we give thanks. Amen and amen.

---

1. Conversation between Jerry Falwell and Pat Robertson, *The PTL Club*, September 13, 2001.

2. Richard Rohr, *Falling Upward: A Spirituality for the Two Halves of Life* (San Francisco: Josey-Bass, 2011), p. 138.

Lent 4
Luke 15:1-3, 11b-32

Now all the tax collectors and sinners were coming near to listen to him. And the Pharisees and the scribes were grumbling and saying, "This fellow welcomes sinners and eats with them." So he told them this parable... Then Jesus said, "There was a man who had two sons. The younger of them said to his father, 'Father, give me the share of the property that will belong to me.' So he divided his property between them. A few days later the younger son gathered all he had and traveled to a distant country, and there he squandered his property in dissolute living. When he had spent everything, a severe famine took place throughout that country, and he began to be in need. So he went and hired himself out to one of the citizens of that country, who sent him to his fields to feed the pigs. He would gladly have filled himself with the pods that the pigs were eating; and no one gave him anything. But when he came to himself he said, 'How many of my father's hired hands have bread enough and to spare, but here I am dying of hunger! I will get up and go to my father, and I will say to him, "Father, I have sinned against heaven and before you; I am no longer worthy to be called your son; treat me like one of your hired hands." ' So he set off and went to his father. But while he was still far off, his father saw him and was filled with compassion; he ran and put his arms around him and kissed him. Then the son said to him, 'Father, I have sinned against heaven and before you; I am no longer worthy to be called your son.' But the father said to his slaves, 'Quickly, bring out a robe — the best one — and put it on him; put a ring on his finger and sandals on his feet. And get the fatted calf and kill it, and let us eat and celebrate; for this son of mine was dead and is alive again; he was lost and is found!' " And they began to celebrate. "Now his elder son was in the field; and when he came and approached the house, he heard music and dancing. He called one of the slaves and asked what was going on. He replied, 'Your brother has come, and your father has killed the fatted calf, because he has got him back safe and sound.' Then he became angry and refused to go in. His father came out and began to plead with him. But he answered his father, 'Listen! For all these years I have been working like a slave for you, and I have never disobeyed your command; yet you have never given me even a young goat so that I might celebrate with my friends. But when this son of yours came back, who has devoured your property with prostitutes, you killed the fatted calf for him!' Then the father said to him, 'Son, you are always with me, and all that is mine is yours. But we had to celebrate and rejoice, because this brother of yours was dead and has come to life; he was lost and has been found.' "

BLAGO AND RADNAN, TWO LOST SONS

The topic of today's gospel reading is the very familiar parable of the prodigal son. It is found in Luke 15 and immediately follows the parables of the lost sheep and the lost coin. In the first few verses of this chapter, Luke gave us the context. The scribes and Pharisees in Jesus' audience were grumbling. "This fellow welcomes sinners and eats with them."

To paraphrase Jesus' response, "Well, of course, I welcome and associate with sinners. They are the ones lost to God. When a woman with ten silver coins misplaces a coin, will she not search for it until she finds it? And when she finds it will she not call all the neighbors and tell them how excited she is? In that same way, there is great joy among the angels when one sinner repents.

"Or when one not-too-bright sheep wanders off will not a caring shepherd leave the rest of flock untended to search for that lost one until he finds it? Will he not put the found sheep on his shoulders and dance back to the rest of the flock whistling a happy tune? In heaven, there is more rejoicing over one repentant sinner than over a multitude of the righteous who have no need of repentance" (vv. 3-10).

Frankly, I don't think the scribes and Pharisees would have been particularly impressed by Jesus' response to their grumbling. Certainly they would have noted the obvious problems with these stories. It would be a terrible mistake for that woman to tell neighbors about replenishing her household stack of silver coins. Common sense dictates that when you have a fortune in silver in the house, it is best kept a secret. If you don't want burglarized, don't tell anyone. And consider the foolishness of leaving 99 sheep to find and return a wanderer. That would be irresponsible. A competent shepherd does not leave the flock defenseless and exposed to the dangers of the wilderness and the ravages of predators.

Because of these problems, the noted writer, Frederick Buechner suggested that these parables are best understood as having an element of humor.[1] Jesus, as every other great storyteller, knew the value of comedy. An unpleasant truth will slide down more easily when lubricated by laughter. To make his case for how God's extravagant love accomplished improbable things with impossible people, Jesus added a dash of comedic hyperbole.

Let me remind you again of the context. The scribes and Pharisees grumbled. "This fellow welcomes sinners and eats with them." This complaining came from people who should have been natural allies of Jesus, not his enemies. While a case can be made that they were not particularly likeable, scribes and Pharisees, in first-century Palestine, set the gold standard for religiosity. More than other groups, they were the ones who wanted to serve God. For that reason, Jesus wanted them to understand why he associated with sinners.

When the stories about the lost coin and lost sheep failed to accomplish that, Jesus told a third parable on the same topic. We call it the parable of the prodigal son, but that is really not fully descriptive. I think it is more accurate to call it the parable of the two lost sons. It is among the best loved stories in scripture. Unfortunately, the sharp edges of meaning have been worn smooth by the retelling. In order to highlight some of that meaning, I will tell the story from a different perspective. There is a chance you will not like my story.

In fact, you may be irritated. That is perfectly all right. The way Jesus told the story irritated the scribes and Pharisees.

Once upon a time there was a dysfunctional family composed of Radnan, a troublesome younger son who posed a serious challenge to his father; Blago, a dutiful older brother who did everything his father asked; Yakob, their father whose compassion and understanding had no limits; and, we assume, a wife and mother who never gets mentioned in the story. The family lived on the cul-de-sac of a quiet street in a residential area of a large city.

As you might guess from their names, they have not always lived in that house. When Blago was a toddler and Radnan an infant, the family emigrated from one of those small eastern European countries with a long name. They came with almost no money. Their assets were limited to a love of family, a willingness to work hard, and an unshakeable confidence in the value of honesty and integrity. For years they lived in a basement apartment in the urban core. To support the family, Yakob mowed lawns or shoveled snow during daylight hours and worked midnight to morning at a local bodega. It took several years, but Yakob saved a down payment and secured a loan to buy a gas station and convenience store on a freeway exit.

Even as the family ascended the ladder of financial achievement and community respect, Yakob preached to his sons the importance of being honest in business, of never doing anything to bring shame to the family, of working hard, and of playing by the rules. By the time Blago and Radnan were young adults, the family owned five combination gas station and convenience stores at exits along the city's freeways. Then they bought that house on the cul-de-sac of a quiet street.

Life was good for Yakob and his family until trouble came. Radnan, the always headstrong younger brother, went into full rebellion. One day he said, "Dad, I am getting tired of waiting around for you to die. I want my share of the inheritance now."

A typical father might have responded, "And I want you to go over to the gas station at Exit 118 and clean the restrooms. Now, take a guess at which one of us is more likely to get what he

51

wants?" That didn't happen because Yakob was not a typical parent. His answer to his son's world-class chutzpah *defies common sense. Yakob emptied his savings account and sold a couple of gas stations in order to fill Radnan's request.*

Predictably, as soon as the money was deposited in his newly opened bank account, Radnan headed for a distant city. He put a down payment on an expensive sports car and rented an apartment in a complex advertising "Swinging Singles Only." To better fit in, he told people that his name was Randy, not Radnan. In this new life, he hosted wild parties nearly every night. At those parties, Randy funded copious amounts of free food, free alcohol, and illegal drugs at discounted prices. Needless to say, those seeking to benefit from Randy's generosity flocked to him as house flies to honey.

In eighteen months, Randy's entire inheritance was gone. The bank repossessed his sports car. The apartment manager evicted him. When he stopped paying for the parties, his groupies abandoned him. An economic downturn renders it impossible to find a decent job. He is reduced to sleeping under a bridge and eating from the trash barrels behind fast food restaurants.

One morning while looking for breakfast at the bottom of the dumpster behind Bob's Beefy Burgers, Randy had an epiphany. "This is pathetic," he thought to himself. "I am battling rats and cockroaches to find a half-eaten cheeseburger. It wasn't supposed to be this way. I was going to prove that if I had a pocketful of money I could flourish on my own. I thought I didn't need my father and his traditional ways. I was wrong. I have ruined my life and embarrassed my family. My only hope is to return home, beg my father's forgiveness, and ask for a minimum wage job at one of his gas stations."

For the next couple days, Randy cogitated on how to proceed. It will only make matters worse if I tell my father to call me "Randy" instead of "Radnan," he quickly concluded. He finally decided to write and memorize a little speech. "Father, I have sinned against heaven and have brought shame to you. I am no longer worthy to be called your son. Please treat me like one of your employees." The younger son planned to give this speech before his father was overcome by anger and ordered him away from the front door.

Meanwhile, back at the little house on the quiet cul-de-sac, things had been difficult. Giving Radnan all the money in the savings account created serious cash flow problems. Selling two of the five gas stations meant terminating long-term, beloved employees. To replace the labor of those lost employees, Yakob and Drago worked longer hours for less income. It addition to the financial damage, Radnan embarrassed his father to the point of public humiliation. Through it all, however, the older brother Drago did everything asked of him.

In spite of the shame and disappointment, Yacob still loved Radnan. Every day, Yakob prayed his son would come to his senses and return home. Every morning Yakob opened his computer anticipating an email from his wayward son. Each day, Yakob studied the faces of customers at the gas station hoping to recognize Radnan, his lost son.

It happened in the middle of a summer afternoon. Yakob was home doing paperwork for his businesses. He happened to glance out the front window. Before he saw the face, he recognized that hands-jammed-into-front-pockets, slumped shouldered, hesitant walk of Radnan. Yakob did not wait for the doorbell. He bolted out the front door, down the steps, and through the cul-de-sac toward his son.

Radnan saw his father coming and started into his carefully rehearsed speech. "Father I have sinned against heaven and have brought shame...." Before he could finish, his father threw his arms around him and welcomed him home. Yakob called the deli at his largest combination convenience store and gas station and ordered enough food for a "Welcome Home" party that evening. Yacob raced house to house around the cul-de-sac inviting the neighbors to come.

When the older brother, Drago got home about 9:00 that evening he was startled to hear music playing and to see the neighbors dancing in the street. When he asked, Drago was told it was a party for Radnan. His brother had come home.

Drago was outraged. He located his father and unloaded his anger. "Radnan nearly bankrupted the family. He humiliated you in public. For the past year and half, he lived like a wild animal. He is a sinner and you give him a party. I, on the other hand, stayed and worked. I followed the rules. I did everything right and you never gave me a party."

Yakob tried to explain to Drago. "Son, you are always with me. All I have is yours. We had to celebrate Radnan's return. He was lost and now he is found."

We never get to hear how Drago responded to his father. Did he reject Yacob's explanation for the party or did he understand and join in the rejoicing? We don't know. The parable ends with Drago dumping his anger on Yacob.

What we can assume is that when Drago scolded his father, it hurt Yakob deeply. In fact, Drago's behavior must have cut so deeply the older brother must have been deemed as much a lost sinner as the younger brother. Radnan was lost because he broke the rules of honesty, integrity, and honor for family and for God. He went off to a wicked, distant place and wasted his resources and his life. Drago was the so-called "good person" in the story. He was like the scribes and Pharisees who had been grumbling about Jesus spending time with sinners. He kept all the rules. He believed all the right things. He did all the right things. His only error was failing to grasp the purpose of believing and doing all the things.

A righteous and holy life is not a matter of keeping or not keeping the rules and regulations. A blessed life comes by maintaining open and loving relationships with God, community, family, and neighbor. Faithful living is not a matter of rule keeping. It is a matter of healthy, loving, accepting, relationship building with God and all God's children.

In the parable, the younger brother finally figured it out. The parable never said if the other lost son came home or not. The concern for each of us in this Lenten season of self-examination is to ask which of the brothers are we most like: the one who just complained about the way others fell short or the one who came to understand the truth that faithful living comes in loving relationships?

---

1. Frederick Buechner, *Telling the Truth: The Gospel as Tragedy, Comedy & Fairy Tale* (New York: Harper Collins Publishers, 1977).

Lent 5
John 12:1-8

Six days before the Passover Jesus came to Bethany, the home of Lazarus, whom he had raised from the dead. There they gave a dinner for him. Martha served, and Lazarus was one of those at the table with him. Mary took a pound of costly perfume made of pure nard, anointed Jesus' feet, and wiped them with her hair. The house was filled with the fragrance of the perfume. But Judas Iscariot, one of his disciples (the one who was about to betray him), said, "Why was this perfume not sold for three hundred denarii and the money given to the poor?" (He said this not because he cared about the poor, but because he was a thief; he kept the common purse and used to steal what was put into it.) Jesus said, "Leave her alone. She bought it so that she might keep it for the day of my burial. You always have the poor with you, but you do not always have me."

LENT 5
JOHN 12:1-8

THE DEVASTATING INFLUENCE OF FAULTFINDING, NAY-SAYING, AND NITPICKING

This is the fifth and final Sunday in Lent. In today's gospel reading, it is the Saturday night before a crowd lined the streets of Jerusalem to give Jesus a parade, throw palm branches in his path, and sing, "Hosanna! Blessed is the one who comes in the name of the Lord" (v. 13). In spite of that enthusiastic welcome, by the following Friday night, Jesus was in a grave.

In the previous few weeks, it was increasingly evident that things were headed in that direction. There had been serious run-ins with the religious authorities. Jesus had predicted his death and John told us there was already a plan to make his death a reality (8:21-30; 11:45-56).

On this particular Saturday evening, however, Jesus and the apostles took a respite from worry. They accepted an invitation to dinner in Bethany, a small crossroads village only two miles from Jerusalem (John 11:28). The party was being held at the home of Martha, her sister Mary, and their brother Lazarus. All the people at the party were already acquainted with one another. The evening promised to be one of rest, relaxation, food, and fellowship. Lazarus is an old friend not only of Jesus, but at least a few of the apostles (John 11:31). Not all that long ago, Jesus altered his preaching schedule to go to Bethany and resuscitate Lazarus from the dead. On a different occasion, Jesus stopped for lunch at Martha's house and had a wonderful afternoon of conversation with Mary (Luke 10:38-42).

The evening delivered on its promises. Per usual, the food Martha prepared was delicious. The service was impeccable. The conversation was uplifting. It was a great evening. Before Jesus and the apostles said their "good-byes," Mary slipped quietly out of the room. She returned carrying an incredibly expensive jar of perfume. It was said to be worth nearly a full year's wages (v. 5, footnote *m*). Mary broke the seal on the jar, knelt before Jesus, and washed his feet with the perfume. The gospel tells us the fragrance of the perfume filled the house (v. 3).

That is no benign observation. The smell of the ancient world was strong and offensive. Deodorants were unavailable. Bathing habits fell far short of our standard. There was no weekly garbage pick-up service. Raw sewage flowed down the city streets, not through underground pipes to a city waste treatment facility. Daily life in the ancient world was filled with unpleasant odors.

On that particular night, Mary used perfume to express her thanks to Jesus for the restored life of Lazarus and for the friendship of Jesus. She wanted Jesus to experience the cool, comforting sensations of nard before he resumed his journey toward Golgotha. She accomplished that with this perfume that drove out every trace of bad smell in that room and replaced it with the fragrant scent of angels' breath. You can almost hear singing in the background, "There is a sweet, sweet spirit in this place and I know it is the presence of the Lord."

That holy moment ended abruptly. Judas Iscariot, the apostle who was to betray Jesus, spoke: "Why was this perfume not sold for three hundred denarii and the money given to the poor?" (v. 5). I imagine that remark elicited an audible gasp.

What Judas said had an element of practical truth. Perfume worth a year's salary would buy truckloads of food and clothing for the poor. Stretching out a helping hand to the poor is central to a meaningful practice of one's faith. By any reasonable standard, it was an over-the-top extravagance to spend that much money on foot washing. On the other hand, that truth is beside the point. Although incredibly important, responding to the plight of the poor was not on this particular evening's agenda.

This night was devoted to the physical and spiritual renewal of the dinner guests. Mary's gesture was a magnanimous act of love and thanksgiving. In spite of the truth in Judas' comment, what, when, and how he made his point belittled Mary's thoughtful gesture and transformed the mood at the dinner. The fragrant scent of a sweet, sweet spirit was sucked out of the room and replaced by the stench of moldy blanket faultfinding.

This is not the only time Jesus experienced a negative comment destroying a special moment. Consider an event recorded in Luke 4. On a weekend visit to his hometown of Nazareth, Jesus went to the synagogue for worship. When asked to speak, our Lord read a short passage from the book of Isaiah that began, "The Spirit of the Lord is upon me, because he has anointed me to bring good news to the poor." When finished, Jesus rerolled the scroll, handed it back to the attendant, sat down, and preached a brief homily on how that passage applied to him. Luke said very explicitly that "all spoke well of him (Jesus) and were amazed at the gracious words that came from his mouth."

Almost immediately this "Welcome Home Jesus" atmosphere was interrupted by a fellow sitting on the back pew. (To paraphrase) "Hey, just hold on a minute. Isn't that the guy who grew up on Carpenter Street? Isn't he one of Joseph's kids? I think I remember he played on the same Little

League team with my son. Who does he think he is? How does he think he can lay claim to the prophecy of Isaiah? This Jesus is just like every other kid who grew up in Nazareth. There is nothing special about him."

There ensued a brief back and forth conversation between Jesus and the audience. In a matter of minutes the attitude of the people in the synagogue went from wonderful to terrible. Those who "spoke well of him and were amazed at the gracious words that came from his mouth" transmogrified into a mob "filled with rage." These angry people threatened to throw Jesus off a cliff at the edge of the city. Such was the devastating possibility of one person making an offhand, negative, faultfinding remark.

This is still an issue in our time. All of us have been in situations where someone played the part of the Judas at the dinner party in Bethany or the guy in the back pew at the Nazareth synagogue. These are the faultfinders who love to point out what is wrong with every person, idea, and situation. These are the nitpickers who complain about a mole hill problem until it becomes a mountain.

Collectively, I call these folks the "aginners." It doesn't matter what it is, they are "agin" it. "Aginners" are in every family, every church, every place of employment, and every neighborhood. In advanced years they can be identified as the ones who grumble, "In my life I have seen thousands of changes and I have been 'agin' every one of them."

Among the most readily identified groups who are really good at being negative are the talking heads on cable news, the familiar voices of talk radio, as well as those who use websites and social media as platforms to launch attacks on people and ideas they do not like. They come from across the political and ideological spectrum. Each in his or her way applies invective to mock, belittle, and even mischaracterize the worldviews, political opinions, and lifestyles of those who offend them. This group not only seems to understand the devastating influence of nay-saying, faultfinding, and nitpicking, it is their stock in trade. Unfortunately, their collective intolerance contributes significantly to damaging the social fabric that holds us together as a people. The vast majority of those who are good at faultfinding, nay-saying, and nitpicking do not gain public notoriety. They are everyday people who just happen to be good at making negative comments. Sometimes they don't seem to fully understand the influence they have. In fact, sometimes I am not certain they are even aware they are "aginners."

I once knew a minister who was an "aginner." Our paths crossed frequently in ministerial retreats, meetings, conferences, workshops, and social settings. This fellow had a remarkable ability to faultfind and nitpick. To illustrate, when a speaker finished and opened the meeting for questions, this fellow always had something to say. Seldom were any of his comments positive. Instead, he liked to point out factual errors and correct for omissions in the speaker's presentation. He was very well-read. Consequently, he loved to articulate a counterpoint to the speaker's point. He also had a remarkable ability to spot the flaw in the speaker's thesis.

When I first met this fellow, I was enamored by what I considered his intelligence and analytical powers. In time I realized that being an "aginner" requires no special skill. We live in an imperfect world filled with imperfect people. Every person, idea, and plan is less than perfect. Something is always wrong. It doesn't take any special gift to point that out. "Aginners" only tear things down, turn enthusiasm into carping, and poison the well with negative their commentary. Nitpicking, nay-saying, faultfinders seldom participate in the far more demanding task of making a positive contribution.

This minister was always polite. He was not arrogant or angry in his demeanor. He didn't seem to hunger for the group's attention. Rather than malevolent he seemed motivated only to perform a helpful service for the speaker and the group. I certainly do not think he set out to join the ranks of Judas at the dinner party in Bethany or the fellow on the back pew in Nazareth. Yet that is exactly what he did.

So how do we deal with the devastating influence of naysaying, nitpicking, and faultfinding? Let me suggest three important principles.

First, don't underestimate the enormous amount of power wielded by the "aginner." With a raised eyebrow or a demeaning comment, a nasty letter to the editor, or a derogatory anonymous letter, an "aginner" can blow a worthwhile idea out of the water. He can suck the air out of the most self-confident person. She can turn a crowd from cheering to jeering with an off-hand remark. Do not underestimate the power of the negative.

Second, beware that you and your words have that same power on other people. Your off-hand, unthinking remarks can be devastating to others. All of us are capable of saying things to people who love and respect us that hurt and demoralize them. We can justify it by claiming we were acting in that person's best interest. However, we need to keep in mind this unwelcome principle of our humanness. A negative comment delivered by someone loved and respected carries ten times the power of a positive comment. That means that in our relationships with those closest to us, just to keep things in proper balance, we need to be giving ten positive comments for every negative one. Never underestimate the devastating influence of faultfinding, nitpicking, and nay-saying.

Third, resist the temptation to establish your worth or your authority by being an "aginner." It is an easy expertise to develop, but it contributes very little to the common good.

We interact with "aginners" on an almost every day basis. They are all around us. From time to time, most of us perform that function. We cannot do away with the authority of the "aginner," but we can minimize it by being aware of the power we give to it.

And may God grant to each of us the strength and wisdom to avoid joining the ranks of Judas and all the other unrestrained "aginners." Instead may we seek and practice the wisdom of Proverbs (16:24): "Pleasant words are like a honeycomb, sweetness to the soul and health to the body."

Oh Lord, may it be so. Amen and amen.

Passion / Palm Sunday
Luke 22:14—23:56

When the hour came, he took his place at the table, and the apostles with him. He said to them, "I have eagerly desired to eat this Passover with you before I suffer; for I tell you, I will not eat it until it is fulfilled in the kingdom of God." Then he took a cup, and after giving thanks he said, "Take this and divide it among yourselves; for I tell you that from now on I will not drink of the fruit of the vine until the kingdom of God comes." Then he took a loaf of bread, and when he had given thanks, he broke it and gave it to them, saying, "This is my body, which is given for you. Do this in remembrance of me." And he did the same with the cup after supper, saying, "This cup that is poured out for you is the new covenant in my blood. But see, the one who betrays me is with me, and his hand is on the table. For the Son of Man is going as it has been determined, but woe to that one by whom he is betrayed!" Then they began to ask one another, which one of them it could be who would do this. A dispute also arose among them as to which one of them was to be regarded as the greatest. But he said to them, "The kings of the Gentiles lord it over them; and those in authority over them are called benefactors. But not so with you; rather the greatest among you must become like the youngest, and the leader like one who serves. For who is greater, the one who is at the table or the one who serves? Is it not the one at the table? But I am among you as one who serves. You are those who have stood by me in my trials; and I confer on you, just as my Father has conferred on me, a kingdom, so that you may eat and drink at my table in my kingdom, and you will sit on thrones judging the twelve tribes of Israel. Simon, Simon, listen! Satan has demanded to sift all of you like wheat, but I have prayed for you that your own faith may not fail;

and you, when once you have turned back, strengthen your brothers." And he said to him, "Lord, I am ready to go with you to prison and to death!" Jesus said, "I tell you, Peter, the cock will not crow this day, until you have denied three times that you know me." He said to them, "When I sent you out without a purse, bag, or sandals, did you lack anything?" They said, "No, not a thing." He said to them, "But now, the one who has a purse must take it, and likewise a bag. And the one who has no sword must sell his cloak and buy one. For I tell you, this scripture must be fulfilled in me, 'And he was counted among the lawless'; and indeed what is written about me is being fulfilled." They said, "Lord, look, here are two swords." He replied, "It is enough." He came out and went, as was his custom, to the Mount of Olives; and the disciples followed him. When he reached the place, he said to them, "Pray that you may not come into the time of trial." Then he withdrew from them about a stone's throw, knelt down, and prayed, "Father, if you are willing, remove this cup from me; yet, not my will but yours be done." Then an angel from heaven appeared to him and gave him strength. In his anguish he prayed more earnestly, and his sweat became like great drops of blood falling down on the ground. When he got up from prayer, he came to the disciples and found them sleeping because of grief, and he said to them, "Why are you sleeping? Get up and pray that you may not come into the time of trial." While he was still speaking, suddenly a crowd came, and the one called Judas, one of the twelve, was leading them. He approached Jesus to kiss him; but Jesus said to him, "Judas, is it with a kiss that you are betraying the Son of Man?" When those who were around him saw what was coming, they asked, "Lord, should we strike with the sword?" Then one of them struck the slave of the high priest and cut off his right ear. But Jesus said, "No more of this!" And he touched his ear and healed him. Then Jesus said to the chief priests, the officers of the temple police, and the elders who had come for him, "Have you come out with swords and clubs as if I were a bandit? When I was with you day after day in the temple, you did not lay hands on me. But this is your hour, and the power of darkness!" Then they seized him and led him away, bringing him into the high priest's house. But Peter was following at a distance. When they had kindled a fire in the middle of the courtyard and sat down together, Peter sat among them. Then a servant-girl, seeing him in the firelight, stared at him and said, "This man also was with him." But he denied it, saying, "Woman, I do not know him." A little later someone else, on seeing him, said, "You also are one of them." But Peter said, "Man, I am not!" Then about an hour later still another kept insisting, "Surely this man also was with him; for he is a Galilean." But Peter said, "Man, I do not know what you are talking about!" At that moment, while he was still speaking, the cock crowed. The Lord turned and looked at Peter. Then Peter remembered the word of the Lord, how he had said to him, "Before the cock crows today, you will deny me three times." And he went out and wept bitterly. Now the men who were holding Jesus began to mock him and beat him; they also blindfolded him and kept asking him, "Prophesy! Who is it that struck you?" They kept heaping many other insults on him. When day came, the assembly of the elders of the people, both chief priests and scribes, gathered together, and they brought him to their council. They said, "If you are the Messiah, tell us." He replied, "If I tell you, you will not believe; and if I question you, you will not answer. But from now on the Son of Man will be seated at the right hand of the power of God." All of them asked, "Are you, then, the Son of God?" He said to them, "You say that I am." Then they said, "What further testimony do we need? We have heard it ourselves from his own lips!" ... Then the assembly rose as a body and brought Jesus before Pilate. They began to accuse him, saying, "We found this man perverting our nation, forbidding us to pay taxes to the emperor, and saying that he himself is the Messiah, a king." Then Pilate asked him, "Are you the king of the Jews?" He answered, "You say so." Then Pilate said to the chief priests and the crowds, "I find no basis for an accusation against this man." But they were insistent and said, "He stirs up the people by teaching throughout all Judea, from Galilee where he began even to this place." When Pilate heard this, he asked whether the man was a Galilean. And when he learned that he was under Herod's jurisdiction, he sent him off to Herod, who was himself in Jerusalem at that time. When Herod saw Jesus, he was very glad, for he had been wanting to see him for a long time, because he had heard about him and was hoping to see him perform some sign. He questioned him at some length, but Jesus gave him no answer. The chief priests and the scribes stood by, vehemently accusing him. Even Herod with his soldiers treated him with contempt and mocked him; then he put an elegant robe on him, and sent him back to Pilate. That same day Herod and Pilate became friends with each other; before this they had been enemies. Pilate then called together the chief priests, the leaders, and the people, and said to them, "You brought me this man as one who was perverting the people; and here I have examined him in your presence and have not found this man guilty of any of your charges against him. Neither has Herod, for he sent him back to us. Indeed, he has done nothing to deserve death. I will therefore have him flogged and release him." Then they all shouted out together, "Away with this fellow! Release Barabbas for us!" (This was a man who had been put in prison for an insurrection that had taken place in the city, and for murder.) Pilate, wanting to release Jesus, addressed them again;

but they kept shouting, "Crucify, crucify him!" A third time he said to them, "Why, what evil has he done? I have found in him no ground for the sentence of death; I will therefore have him flogged and then release him." But they kept urgently demanding with loud shouts that he should be crucified; and their voices prevailed. So Pilate gave his verdict that their demand should be granted. He released the man they asked for, the one who had been put in prison for insurrection and murder, and he handed Jesus over as they wished. As they led him away, they seized a man, Simon of Cyrene, who was coming from the country, and they laid the cross on him, and made him carry it behind Jesus. A great number of the people followed him, and among them were women who were beating their breasts and wailing for him. But Jesus turned to them and said, "Daughters of Jerusalem, do not weep for me, but weep for yourselves and for your children. For the days are surely coming when they will say, 'Blessed are the barren, and the wombs that never bore, and the breasts that never nursed.' Then they will begin to say to the mountains, 'Fall on us'; and to the hills, 'Cover us.' For if they do this when the wood is green, what will happen when it is dry?" Two others also, who were criminals, were led away to be put to death with him. When they came to the place that is called The Skull, they crucified Jesus there with the criminals, one on his right and one on his left. Then Jesus said, "Father, forgive them; for they do not know what they are doing." And they cast lots to divide his clothing. And the people stood by, watching; but the leaders scoffed at him, saying, "He saved others; let him save himself if he is the Messiah of God, his chosen one!" The soldiers also mocked him, coming up and offering him sour wine, and saying, "If you are the King of the Jews, save yourself!" There was also an inscription over him, "This is the King of the Jews." One of the criminals who were hanged there kept deriding him and saying, "Are you not the Messiah? Save yourself and us!" But the other rebuked him, saying, "Do you not fear God, since you are under the same sentence of condemnation? And we indeed have been condemned justly, for we are getting what we deserve for our deeds, but this man has done nothing wrong." Then he said, "Jesus, remember me when you come into your kingdom." He replied, "Truly I tell you, today you will be with me in Paradise." It was now about noon, and darkness came over the whole land until three in the afternoon, while the sun's light failed; and the curtain of the temple was torn in two. Then Jesus, crying with a loud voice, said, "Father, into your hands I commend my spirit." Having said this, he breathed his last. When the centurion saw what had taken place, he praised God and said, "Certainly this man was innocent." And when all the crowds who had gathered there for this spectacle saw what had taken place, they returned home, beating their breasts. But all his acquaintances, including the women who had followed him from Galilee, stood at a distance, watching these things. Now there was a good and righteous man named Joseph, who, though a member of the council, had not agreed to their plan and action. He came from the Jewish town of Arimathea, and he was waiting expectantly for the kingdom of God. This man went to Pilate and asked for the body of Jesus. Then he took it down, wrapped it in a linen cloth, and laid it in a rock-hewn tomb where no one had ever been laid. It was the day of Preparation, and the sabbath was beginning. The women who had come with him from Galilee followed, and they saw the tomb and how his body was laid. Then they returned, and prepared spices and ointments. On the sabbath they rested according to the commandment.

PASSION / PALM SUNDAY
LUKE 22:14—23:56

FROM DEEP
UNTO DEEP

On the Christian calendar, today begins the last week of Lent.[1] The forty days between Shrove Tuesday, at the end of Mardi Gras, and the Saturday before Easter are intended as a time for prayer, meditation, reflection, and repentance. Generally speaking, the serious nature of Lent makes it emotionally a rather dreary time. During Holy Week, the mood moves from dreary to downright lugubrious.

Next Sunday morning, of course, we will awake to the joyous news that "Christ the Lord is risen today. Alleluia! He is risen indeed." We are not, however, there as yet. To get to Easter, we have to go through the events that led up to the resurrection. The point I want to make this morning is that the difficult journey through this week has the potential to drive our spiritual lives from deep unto deep.

Things seem to get off to a good start. On the Sunday prior to Easter, the one we observe today, there was a parade. When Jesus and his traveling entourage arrived in Jerusalem the crowd welcomed our Lord as though he was a conquering hero. "Hosanna to the king of kings, blessed is he who comes in the name of the Lord." The multitudes shouted and sang and threw palm branches in his path. The apostles and other close followers of the Lord had been worried about this trip. "Stay here in Galilee" they had pleaded. "The Galileans know and love you, Jesus. Jerusalem has mean streets." They warned Jesus of sworn enemies and sinister plots that lurked in the narrow alleys and broad boulevards of the capital city. That Sunday morning's welcoming palm parade ameliorated their fears. Those who had raised the alarm must have thought they were wrong. "These sophisticated big city folks love Jesus as much as we do."

The good feeling did not last long. For whatever reason, Jesus insisted on getting in the face of the establishment. The apostles barely had time to return the borrowed donkey Jesus had ridden in the parade, when the Lord went to the great temple and began to irritate powerful people. He overturned the tables of the moneychangers and set free the goats and sheep that were to be sold for sacrifice. For heaven sake, he even released the pigeons from their cages. On Sunday they gave our Lord a parade, but by Tuesday and Wednesday Jesus repeatedly stood on a curb in the city market preaching sermons that mocked the authority of scribes and Pharisees.

When Jesus and his closest followers gathered for that Thursday night dinner, it was intended as a respite from the stress the week had become. Everyone else wanted to get away from it all, but Jesus insisted on discussing betrayal and dying. "One of you has already betrayed me and the rest will run way when the going gets tough." Peter, ever the self-assured, objected, "Lord the rest of them may do that, but I will not. I will never fail you." Jesus shook his head, "Peter, before the sun comes up tomorrow morning, you will deny me three times."

It was intended to be an agreeable dinner party, but the mood was soured when Jesus brought up the coming betrayal of Judas and predicted Peter's denial. After dinner, the group sang a hymn together. Jesus took a couple of his dearest friends to pray with him in the Garden of Gethsemane. The route from where they were having that last meal to the prayer garden was and still is a simple one. Take any gate on the south side of the ancient walled city of Jerusalem; follow the

Jericho Road across the Kidron Valley to the Mount of Olives. The Garden of Gethsemane is partway up the steep hill.

Jesus' experience in the quiet garden of prayer was marked by anguish. Those trusted apostles had the attention spans of small children. They lost interest and fell asleep. How disappointed Jesus was in them. "Could you not even stay awake with me?"

The master knew where this night was headed and he was not looking forward to it. He prayed, "Lord, let this cup pass from me." That's a polite way to say, "God, I don't want to do this. Judas Iscariot and Simon Peter have been good and loyal friends. I don't want Judas to betray me. I don't want Peter to deny he ever knew me. God of heaven and earth, I have thought about this very carefully and all things considered I don't want to be arrested, beaten, tortured, and hung on a cross to die. Lord, let this cup pass from me."

God did not answer Jesus' prayer, at least not the way Jesus asked to have it answered. Less than 24 hours after praying "let this cup pass from me," Jesus was dead and buried.

We know the story did not end there. After the grave came the resurrection. With all of you, I look forward to Easter and its promise of new life. That, however, doesn't happen until next week. This week we call "Holy" is a series of disappointing, agonizing, terrible events. Before we get to Easter we have to go through the master getting arrested in the Garden of Gethsemane; Peter denying he even knew Jesus; the questioning in the basement torture chamber of Caiaphas, the high priest; the sham trial at the palace of Pontius Pilate; the disappointment when some of those who sang "Hosanna to the King of kings" demanded Jesus' crucifixion. Before the glory of Easter, Jesus must carry his cross on the Way of Tears. He must be nailed to that cross on Golgotha. Before Easter, our Lord must be placed in the borrowed tomb of Joseph of Arimathea.

I sometimes wish we could skip over all the bad news of Holy Week and go right to the good news of Easter. However, we cannot do that. In order to get to the joy of resurrection and victory, there first must be death and defeat. Without the cross, the empty tomb makes no sense. Moving our spiritual lives from deep unto deep depends on grasping the significance of how the struggles of Holy Week are followed by the certainty of Resurrection Sunday. This journey takes us from the darkness of Holy Week to the light of Easter; from sadness to joy; from defeat to victory; from death to life.

As a child, you learned from experience that the darkness of midnight inevitably will give way to the light of the morning. In your spiritual life, you can be just as certain that inevitable disappointments and struggles will give way to God's grace and love. Believe this: When you are in a pit of despair, don't give up hope. God brings new life into the darkest moments of what otherwise may seem a hopeless situation. Believe that with confident certainty. Doing so makes a difference.

On January 15, 1974, Charley Otera, a fifteen-year-old teenager, returned to his Wichita, Kansas, home after school to discover that both of his parents, plus a brother and a sister, ages 9 and 11, had been murdered. That discovery was a terrible event in the life of a fifteen-year-old kid. Those four members of the Otera family were the first victims of a serial killer who named himself for his method of murder — BTK: bind, torture, and kill.

In 2004, thirty years after the teenage Charley Otera found his family murdered, Wichita police arrested Dennis Rader and charged him with the murders. Charley Otera was interviewed on television the next day. He was now well into his forties and life had not treated him gently. Charlie described the experience in 1974 as "the day my life ended." He went on to say the first thing he did was to give up all religious faith. "I just couldn't believe any more in any God who would let a thing like that happen." He described his life since then as one of unrelenting despair and hopelessness.

Charley Otera's life stalled on his personal Good Friday, January 15, 1974 — a day of suffering and death. Charley never opened himself to even the possibility of Easter and his life was never put back together. I understand how and even why he cut himself off from God and from hope. I understand why, but I contend he did not have to do that. What he did was both sad and unnecessary.

Many years ago, Raymond Gaylord was the senior minister of a congregation in Grand Rapids, Michigan. My wife and I were members of that church when Raymond saw gifts for ministry in me that I had not noticed. He encouraged me to consider ministry, asked me to teach Sunday school, and hired me to direct the church's youth group. Eventually he steered me to seminary and pastoral ministry.

Raymond's son, Jonathan, was a seventeen-year-old high school student. He had his first job at the local hardware store. One evening after work Jonathan was headed to a basketball game at the local high school. He hit a patch of ice on the road, spun out of control, and had a head-on collision with one of the deacon's in the church where his father was pastor. Jonathan was killed instantly.

The family was devastated. Raymond's grief was palpable. His eldest son was dead. There was no explanation that made any sense. There were no easy words of comfort that could ease the pain. The total darkness of Good Friday settled over Raymond and his family. I was a young man at the time. I had almost no training as a theological interpreter of life. For that matter, I didn't have that much experience in life itself. I wondered how my friend Raymond was going to be able to continue in ministry after his son's senseless death. Raymond had given his life in service of God and God rewarded him with tragedy. Because I didn't know how I would react, I worried that Raymond's faith might be destroyed.

A few weeks after Jonathan was killed, a package arrived for Raymond in the mail. It was a gift from one of Raymond's friends, a professor in a nearby seminary. In a handsome wooden frame was a beautiful needlepoint of the Bible verse, Job 13:15 (KJV): "Though (God) slay me, yet will I trust him."

In my youthful exuberance and still quite immature faith, I concluded that gift was not only inappropriate, it was downright hurtful. "The man's son just died and some seminary professor sent him a pious Bible verse on how he should trust God in spite of God's obvious indifference. Where was God when Raymond's son was sliding across the highway into the path of that oncoming car? Job 13:15 seemed to advocate that Raymond should swallow his grief, anger, and disappointment and just trust God. What a cruel, thoughtless thing to do. 'Though he slay me, yet will I trust him' indeed."

Imagine my surprise when Raymond found that verse comforting. In fact, in years to come he said he found it was that verse that did the most to get him through those terrible days of grief.

As my faith has grown, I have come to understand. Raymond Gaylord, like Charley Otera, had an experience of Good Friday that was not unlike the Good Friday from the apostles' perspective — an experience of disappointment, death, and despair. Charley gave up all hope. For thirty years, he had continued in despair. Charley never got past Good Friday. Raymond had a Good Friday experience, but he resolved not to remain there. He opened himself to the possibility of Easter Sunday. Raymond recommitted himself to ministry. He decided that he was not going to let his son

78

die in vain. The congregation he served bought a youth camp and named it for Jonathan. Raymond used his personal grief and suffering to become an instrument of God's healing to other parents who have lost children.

Actually, the King James Version does not state the meaning of Job 13:15 as clearly as it might. Perhaps it is better stated that "I have no hope, yet I have hope in God." When something happens to us that is similar to what happened to Charley Otera and Raymond Gaylord, we cannot look inside ourselves and find the strength and hope and trust we need to get through it. We can however, find hope in God. We have no other place to turn. On this particular week of the church calendar we see this truth demonstrated very clearly. We also experience this truth often in our lives.

When we see no particular reason to hope, we can put our hope in God.

---

1. The gospel reading for this week, Luke 22:14—23:56, covers events from Maundy Thursday to the burial of Jesus. Rather than limiting itself to that period, this sermon addresses all the events of Holy Week. Scripture references come from other gospels and are usually paraphrased in order to weave a narrative of what happened in this week leading to the resurrection.

Maundy Thursday
John 13:1-17, 31b-35

Now before the festival of the Passover, Jesus knew that his hour had come to depart from this world and go to the Father. Having loved his own who were in the world, he loved them to the end. The devil had already put it into the heart of Judas son of Simon Iscariot to betray him. And during supper Jesus, knowing that the Father had given all things into his hands, and that he had come from God and was going to God, got up from the table, took off his outer robe, and tied a towel around himself. Then he poured water into a basin and began to wash the disciples' feet and to wipe them with the towel that was tied around him. He came to Simon Peter, who said to him, "Lord, are you going to wash my feet?" Jesus answered, "You do not know now what I am doing, but later you will understand." Peter said to him, "You will never wash my feet." Jesus answered, "Unless I wash you, you have no share with me." Simon Peter said to him, "Lord, not my feet only but also my hands and my head!" Jesus said to him, "One who has bathed does not need to wash, except for the feet, but is entirely clean. And you are clean, though not all of you." For he knew who was to betray him; for this reason he said, "Not all of you are clean." After he had washed their feet, had put on his robe, and had returned to the table, he said to them, "Do you know what I have done to you? You call me Teacher and Lord — and you are right, for that is what I am. So if I, your Lord and Teacher, have washed your feet, you also ought to wash one another's feet. For I have set you an example, that you also should do as I have done to you. Very truly, I tell you, servants are not greater than their master, nor are messengers greater than the one who sent them. If you know these things, you are blessed if you do them...." When he had gone out, Jesus said, "Now the Son of Man has been glorified, and God has been glorified in him. If God has been glorified in him, God will also glorify him in himself and will glorify him at once. Little children, I am with you only a little longer. You will look for me; and as I said to the Jews so now I say to you, 'Where I am going, you cannot come.' I give you a new commandment, that you love one another. Just as I have loved you, you also should love one another. By this everyone will know that you are my disciples, if you have love for one another."

WHAT WILL WE DO
WHEN HE IS GONE?

John Dickinson understood the importance of being attentive to details. As an elected leader of his local congregation John insisted every decision of the church board follow proper procedure. As the in-house attorney for a small insurance company in a mid-western city, he paid close attention to every word in every corporate contract and insurance policy. John believed that there was a right and a wrong way to do everything. Consequently, he insisted that everything be done "decently and in good order."

Needless to say, these scrupulous practices extended to his family life. For instance, when first married, John sat down one evening with his new wife and guided her through a stack of important papers — Last Will and Testament, insurance policies, bank information, and so forth. For decades, every time John went on a business trip he placed a sealed envelope containing important papers on the top of his bedroom chest-of-drawers. On the front of the envelope it said: "Should the need arise, this will tell you what you need to know and what you need to do." When he returned from out-of-town, John always placed the envelope back under the clothes in the bottom drawer of his dresser. About twice a year, he reviewed and updated the information. As the years passed, the envelope grew thicker.

After the first few years of marriage, his wife didn't pay much attention to this ritual. John handled all their finances.

She trusted him to do what was right and proper. She had no particular interest in the family finances. His wife considered the envelope just another of her husband's endearing behaviors.

In the year of their 47th wedding anniversary, John went to a meeting of the Board of Trustees for his university. As the trustee chair of one of the board committees, he made his report and then asked to be excused. He said he was not feeling well. While returning to his hotel room, John collapsed and died of a massive heart attack.

In the midst of their shock and grief, the family opened the envelope with the note on the front: "Should the need arise, this will tell you what you need to know and what you need to do." The envelope contained details about investments, savings and checking accounts, insurance policies, John's Last Will and Testament, and an inventory of the safe deposit box with directions of where to find the key. The envelope also contained John's updated obituary for the local newspaper; suggestions for his funeral with specific requests for the songs he wanted played, the suit he wanted to wear, the casket he preferred, and a copy of the deed to a cemetery lot. John had also included a note for the family clarifying that these were simply his suggestions. If they so decided, they were free to make other arrangements.

As one might anticipate, everything in that envelope was enormously helpful. It gave the family a road map for dealing with the practical details of his death. John Dickinson did a good thing for his family. I have often recommended people prepare a similar envelope of pertinent information.

Of course John's "should the need arise" envelope addressed only finances and funeral arrangements. As helpful as that was for the family, the information in that envelope did not touch upon deeper spiritual and psychological questions like "Oh, John, how are we going to get along without you?" "How are we going to fill the emptiness created by the loss of your presence in the midst of the daily life of this family?"

I mention this because those are the questions dealt with in today's gospel reading.

This is Thursday of Holy Week. The followers of Jesus were having a last meal together. In the next 24 hours, Jesus would be betrayed, arrested, stand trial, be convicted, and be sentenced to death by crucifixion. As was then common practice, there was no long appeal process. Within hours of his sentencing, Jesus was crucified and buried. The mood in that upper room was, to say the least, somber. Those closest followers of Jesus were filled with a profound sense of impending loss. Each person must have wondered "Oh, Jesus, how are we going to get along without you?"

In the synoptic gospels, Thursday evening's meal is central to the narrative. Matthew, Mark, and Luke remember that Jesus used the bread and wine at the last supper to institute what is variously called the Lord's Supper, the Eucharist, Holy Communion. "This (bread) is my body, which is given for you." "This cup that is poured out for you is the new covenant in my blood."

As often happens, John's gospel offers a different perspective. The fourth gospel discusses the last supper, but more as background. For John, the meal was the setting for Jesus to respond to the apostles' worry about how to get along without him.

John's answer to that question was both simple and profound. To paraphrase the idea: "Here is what we need to do. Love one another and practice that love by serving one another."

In John 13:34-35, Jesus said, "I give you a new commandment, that you love one another. Just as I have loved you, you also should love one another. By this everyone will know that you are my disciples, if you have love for one another."

Of course, this commandment was not particularly new. Jesus had previously spoken of the need to love one another. For that matter, this mandate had been part of the teaching of the Jewish faith for centuries. A call to love had been issued by ancient Greek philosophy. It is even part of some other world religions. "No matter what difficulty we face, if we will just love one another, we will get through."

The mandate to love is ancient, clear, and straightforward. It is not, however, easy to follow. Will Rogers, a comedian and social commentator of the 1920s and '30s, used to say "I never met a man I didn't like."

Will Rogers could say that because he did not know all the people I know. I have met people I didn't like. In fact, I have met some people that I cannot imagine anybody loving or even liking. Yet this mandate remains: "Love one another." The apostles must have asked, "Jesus just how are we supposed to do that?"

Actually, our Lord answered that question a little earlier in the evening. He did so, not so much with his words as by his example. Chapter 13 of John opens by telling us that Jesus knew the time for him to depart from this world was at hand. As the group was eating the last supper together, Jesus took off his outer robe, tied a towel around his waist, poured water in a basin, and humbled himself by washing the feet of the apostles. When he finished Jesus said, as "I have washed your feet, you also ought to wash one another's feet" (v. 14).

Over the centuries, foot washing has become a Maundy (or Holy) Thursday tradition in expressions of Christianity from German Anabaptist to Eastern Orthodox to Ethiopian Coptic to Roman Catholic. To illustrate: When Jorge Mario Bergoglio became the 266th pope, he took the name of

Francis of Assisi, an early thirteenth-century monk who identified with the plight of the poor. Two weeks after he became Pope, on the Thursday of Holy Week 2013, Pope Francis went to the Casal del Marmo, a juvenile detention center in Rome where he demonstrated the ideals of Saint Francis by washing the feet of a dozen adolescent prisoners — including one young Serbian Muslim woman. Pope Francis told those young people "washing your feet means that I am at your service."[1]

"Lord, when you are gone, how will we get through?" The answer is to love one another and to demonstrate that love by serving others. That sentiment is echoed in the famous prayer of Saint Francis of Assisi.

Lord, make me an instrument of thy peace.
Where there is hatred, let me sow love;
Where there is injury, pardon;
Where there is doubt, faith;
Where there is despair, hope;
Where there is darkness, light;
Where there is sadness, joy.
O divine Master, grant that I may not so much seek
To be consoled as to console;
To be understood as to understand;
To be loved as to love.
For it is in giving, that we receive;
It is in pardoning, that we are pardoned;
It is in dying, that we are born to eternal life.

George Matheson was a man who thoroughly understood what it meant to be sustained through great loss by the power of love and the strength that comes from serving others. When Matheson was twenty years of age, he was engaged to a beautiful young woman. At the time, he was studying to be a minister in the Church of Scotland. He started to have some problems with his eyesight and went to see a doctor. He was told he was going blind and in 1862, medicine had nothing to offer. When Matheson told his fiancée, she ended the engagement by telling him she did not want to spend the rest of her life married to a blind man.

He was devastated and could not imagine how he could make it without the love of his fiancée. Fortunately, his unmarried sister offered to take care of him. For two decades, he was supported and sustained by his sister. Her love and service got him through. He finished his training for ministry and eventually became the preaching minister of a large congregation in Edinburgh, Scotland — all while blind.

In 1882, after twenty years of taking care of her brother, that sister fell in love and planned to marry. Her loving attention and support was no longer going to be available to Matheson. He was devastated. The night before the wedding he sat alone, mired in his suffering, wondering "How will I ever get along without her?"

After an hour or so of feeling sorry for himself, he had an epiphany. As a minister of the gospel, he had been called to love others by serving their needs. He would simply continue to do that. By God's grace, he would get through. God's love would sustain him.

That night the blind George Matheson wrote a poem about the strength he gained from that insight. Later the poem was set to music. You may have found strength for your life from these words.

O Love that wilt not let me go,
I rest my weary soul in thee;
I give thee back the life I owe,
That in thine ocean depths its flow
May richer, fuller be.

O light that foll'west all my way,
I yield my flick'ring torch to thee;
My heart restores its borrowed ray,
That in thy sunshine's blaze its day
May brighter, fairer be.

O Joy that seekest me through pain,
I cannot close my heart to thee;
I trace the rainbow through the rain,
And feel the promise is not vain,
That morn shall tearless be.

O Cross that liftest up my head,
I dare not ask to fly from thee;
I lay in dust life's glory dead,
And from the ground there blossoms red
Life that shall endless be.
("O Love That Wilt Not Let Me Go," public domain)

---

1. *New York Daily News* (website), March 30, 2013.

Good Friday
John 18:1—19:42

After Jesus had spoken these words, he went out with his disciples across the Kidron valley to a place where there was a garden, which he and his disciples entered. Now Judas, who betrayed him, also knew the place, because Jesus often met there with his disciples. So Judas brought a detachment of soldiers together with police from the chief priests and the Pharisees, and they came there with lanterns and torches and weapons. Then Jesus, knowing all that was to happen to him, came forward and asked them, "Whom are you looking for?" They answered, "Jesus of Nazareth." Jesus replied, "I am he." Judas, who betrayed him, was standing with them. When Jesus said to them, "I am he," they stepped back and fell to the ground. Again he asked them, "Whom are you looking for?" And they said, "Jesus of Nazareth." Jesus answered, "I told you that I am he. So if you are looking for me, let these men go." This was to fulfill the word that he had spoken, "I did not lose a single one of those whom you gave me." Then Simon Peter, who had a sword, drew it, struck the high priest's slave, and cut off his right ear. The slave's name was Malchus. Jesus said to Peter, "Put your sword back into its sheath. Am I not to drink the cup that the Father has given me?" So the soldiers, their officer, and the Jewish police arrested Jesus and bound him. First they took him to Annas, who was the father-in-law of Caiaphas, the high priest that year. Caiaphas was the one who had advised the Jews that it was better to have one person die for the people. Simon Peter and another disciple followed Jesus. Since that disciple was known to the high priest, he went with Jesus into the courtyard of the high priest, but Peter was standing outside at the gate. So the other disciple, who was known to the high priest, went out, spoke to the woman who guarded the gate, and brought Peter in. The woman said to Peter, "You are not also one of this man's disciples, are you?" He said, "I am not." Now the slaves and the police had made a charcoal fire because it was cold, and they were standing around it and warming themselves. Peter also was standing with them and warming himself. Then the high priest questioned Jesus about his disciples and about his teaching. Jesus answered, "I have spoken openly to the world; I have always taught in synagogues and in the temple, where all the Jews come together. I have said nothing in secret. Why do you ask me? Ask those who heard what I said to them; they know what I said." When he had said this, one of the police standing nearby struck Jesus on the face, saying, "Is that how you answer the high priest?" Jesus answered, "If I have spoken wrongly, testify to the wrong. But if I have spoken rightly, why do you strike me?" Then Annas sent him bound to Caiaphas the high priest. Now Simon Peter was standing and warming himself. They asked him, "You are not also one of his disciples, are you?" He denied it and said, "I am not." One of the slaves of the high priest, a relative of the man whose ear Peter had cut off, asked, "Did I not see you in the garden with him?" Again Peter denied it, and at that moment the cock crowed. Then they took Jesus from Caiaphas to Pilate's headquarters. It was early in the morning. They themselves did not enter the headquarters, so as to avoid ritual defilement and to be able to eat the Passover. So Pilate went out to them and said, "What accusation do you bring against this man?" They answered, "If this man were not a criminal, we would not have handed him over to you." Pilate said to them, "Take him yourselves and judge him according to your law." The Jews replied, "We are not permitted to put anyone to death." (This was to fulfill what Jesus had said when he indicated the kind of death he was to die.) Then Pilate entered the headquarters again, summoned Jesus, and asked him, "Are you the King of the Jews?" Jesus answered, "Do you ask this on your own, or did others tell you about me?" Pilate replied, "I am not a Jew, am I? Your own nation and the chief priests have handed you over to me. What have you done?" Jesus answered, "My kingdom is not from this world. If my kingdom were from this world, my followers would be fighting to keep me from being handed over to the Jews. But as it is, my kingdom is not from here." Pilate asked him, "So you are a king?" Jesus answered, "You say that I am a king. For this I was born, and for this I came into the world, to testify to the truth. Everyone who belongs to the truth listens to my voice." Pilate asked him, "What is truth?" After he had said this, he went out to the Jews again and told them, "I find no case against him. But you have a custom that I release someone for you at the Passover. Do you want me to release for you the King of the Jews?" They shouted in reply, "Not this man, but Barabbas!" Now Barabbas was a bandit. ... Then Pilate took Jesus and had him flogged. And the soldiers wove a crown of thorns and put it on his head, and they dressed him in a purple robe. They kept coming up to him, saying, "Hail, King of the Jews!" and striking him on the face. Pilate went out again and said to them, "Look, I am bringing him out to you to let you know that I find no case against him." So Jesus came out, wearing the crown of thorns and the purple robe. Pilate said to them, "Here is the man!" When the chief priests and the police saw him, they shouted, "Crucify him! Crucify him!" Pilate said to them, "Take him yourselves and crucify him; I find no case against him." The Jews answered him, "We have a law, and according to that law he ought to die because he has claimed to be the Son of God." Now when Pilate heard this, he was more afraid than ever. He entered his headquarters again and asked Jesus, "Where are you from?" But Jesus gave him no answer. Pilate therefore said to him, "Do you refuse to speak to me? Do you not know that I have power to release you, and power to crucify you?" Jesus answered him, "You would have no power over me unless it had been given you from above; therefore the one who handed me over to you is guilty of a greater sin." From then on Pilate tried to release him, but the Jews cried out, "If you release this man, you are *no friend of the emperor. Everyone who claims to be a king sets himself against the emperor." When Pilate heard these words, he brought Jesus outside and sat on the judge's bench at a place called The Stone Pavement, or in Hebrew Gabbatha. Now it was the day of Preparation for the Passover; and it was about noon. He said to the Jews, "Here is your King!" They cried out, "Away with him! Away with him! Crucify him!" Pilate asked them, "Shall I crucify your King?" The chief priests answered, "We have no king but the emperor." Then he handed him over to them to be crucified. So they took Jesus; and carrying the cross by himself, he went out to what is called The Place of the Skull, which in Hebrew is called Golgotha. There they crucified him, and with him two others, one on either side, with Jesus between them. Pilate also had an inscription written and put on the cross. It read, "Jesus of Nazareth, the King of the Jews." Many of the Jews read this inscription, because the place where Jesus was crucified was near the city; and it was written in Hebrew, in Latin, and in Greek. Then the chief priests of the Jews said to Pilate, "Do not write, 'The King of the Jews,' but, 'This man said, I am King of the Jews.' " Pilate answered, "What I have written I have written." When the soldiers had crucified Jesus, they took his clothes and divided them into four parts, one for each soldier. They also took his tunic; now the tunic was seamless, woven in one piece from the top. So they said to one another, "Let us not tear it, but cast lots for it to see who will get it." This was to fulfill what the scripture says, "They divided my clothes among themselves, and for my clothing they cast lots." And that is what the soldiers did. Meanwhile, standing near the cross of Jesus were his mother, and his mother's sister, Mary the wife of Clopas, and Mary Magdalene. When Jesus saw his mother and the disciple whom he loved standing beside her, he said to his mother, "Woman, here is your son." Then he said to the disciple, "Here is your mother." And from that hour the disciple took her into his own home. After this, when Jesus knew that all was now*

*finished, he said (in order to fulfill the scripture), "I am thirsty."
A jar full of sour wine was standing there. So they put a sponge
full of the wine on a branch of hyssop and held it to his mouth.
When Jesus had received the wine, he said, "It is finished."
Then he bowed his head and gave up his spirit. Since it was the
day of Preparation, the Jews did not want the bodies left on the
cross during the sabbath, especially because that sabbath was
a day of great solemnity. So they asked Pilate to have the legs
of the crucified men broken and the bodies removed. Then the
soldiers came and broke the legs of the first and of the other
who had been crucified with him. But when they came to Jesus
and saw that he was already dead, they did not break his legs.
Instead, one of the soldiers pierced his side with a spear, and
at once blood and water came out. (He who saw this has testi-
fied so that you also may believe. His testimony is true, and he
knows that he tells the truth.) These things occurred so that the
scripture might be fulfilled, "None of his bones shall be broken." And again another passage of scripture says, "They will
look on the one whom they have pierced." After these things,
Joseph of Arimathea, who was a disciple of Jesus, though a
secret one because of his fear of the Jews, asked Pilate to let
him take away the body of Jesus. Pilate gave him permission;
so he came and removed his body. Nicodemus, who had at first
come to Jesus by night, also came, bringing a mixture of myrrh
and aloes, weighing about a hundred pounds. They took the
body of Jesus and wrapped it with the spices in linen cloths,
according to the burial custom of the Jews. Now there was a
garden in the place where he was crucified, and in the garden
there was a new tomb in which no one had ever been laid. And
so, because it was the Jewish day of Preparation, and the tomb
was nearby, they laid Jesus there.*

FROM HIS ARREST TO HIS CRUCIFIXION AND BURIAL

It was the last week of July 2013. An ultramodern, high speed passenger train neared the end of a six-hour trip from Madrid to the northwest Spanish city of Ferrol. The train entered a long, steep curve on the outskirts of Santiago de Compostela. Those of us watching the slow motion security camera video realized immediately that this was not going to end well. The train was traveling 120 miles per hour, more than twice the speed limit. About half-way through the curve, a passenger car in the middle of the train began to float off the tracks and drift toward a high concrete, retaining wall. The cars hooked to that errant carriage followed. In a matter of seconds, all of the train's cars were tossed about like so many trash cans in a high wind. Seventy-nine people were killed and 140 were injured.

Every television news program played that video over and over again. It was obvious that from the moment the train started to leave the tracks there was nothing that could be done to avoid the death, destruction, and utter chaos that ensued. Needless to say, there was not an on-time arrival that day in Ferrol, the scheduled destination. Plans were tragically interrupted when the train derailed.

There is a sense in which that is one of the underlying themes in the gospel reading for this Good Friday. John 18:1—19:42 is very long — two full chapters; more than 2,000 words; nearly 10% of the entire gospel of John. It covers events from the betrayal of Jesus by Judas Iscariot in the Garden of Gethsemane to our Lord's interrogation by the high priest to his trial by the Roman governor to his torment at the hands of Roman soldiers to his suffering on the cross to his death and his burial in a garden tomb.

This reading touches on much of what is at the heart of the gospel. Because of its length, we are not going to take the twenty minutes required to read it all aloud. Instead, it is recommended that sometime between now and when you worship on Easter Sunday you read these two chapters as a personal or family devotional. It will be a meaningful spiritual preparation for the glory of Resurrection Sunday.

It is also recommended that as you read you watch for two things. First, notice how John organizes his narrative to demonstrate circumstances going from bad to worse to tragic. Chapter 18 opens in the Garden of Gethsemane when Judas Iscariot made good on his plan to betray Jesus. Judas, the apostolic business administrator, led a gaggle of temple priests, Pharisees, and armed guards from the religion police to the Garden of Gethsemane, where Jesus has gone to pray. The police tried to arrest Jesus. Simon Peter, another of the leading apostles, reacted violently. He took out a knife and cut off the ear of the high priest's slave.

The armed religion police were not deterred by Peter brandishing a deadly weapon. They put Jesus under arrest and took him to be questioned by the high priest. While that interrogation happened in the temple courtyard, Peter waited outside on the street. It was a cold night. A bonfire was built for warmth. Peter joined a group of strangers close to the fire. A few in the crowd thought they recognized Peter. They asked him if he was one of Jesus' followers. Peter denied even knowing the man.

Take note: Judas Iscariot, one of Jesus' closest followers betrayed him to the religion authorities. This was immediately followed by Peter, another in Jesus' inner circle, resorting to bloody violence before denying he was even acquainted with Jesus. Things were not off to a good start.

The interview with the religious authorities went surprisingly well. Even though Jesus took a punch in the face for what was assessed as being disrespectful to the high priest, he made a solid case that he was not guilty of the crime of blasphemy — false religious teaching.

At that point, the religious authorities could have set him free, but they did not. Instead they took Jesus to the secular authority, Pontius Pilate, and told the Roman governor that Jesus had been preaching that he was the king of the Jews. They intended this to be heard as an accusation of treason, a crime against the state.

Jesus' situation had just gotten much more perilous. Rome was tolerant of many things, but treason was not one of them. Anyone guilty of undermining Rome's political authority was likely to meet a swift, cruel death.

It was a surprise when the initial interview with Pontius Pilate went rather well. Pilate had a conversation with Jesus and concluded there was not a case for the charge of treason. Pilate actually went so far as to propose a way to set Jesus free. The Roman governor pointed out that he had a custom of releasing a prisoner as his contribution to the celebration of the Jewish Passover. Pilate offered to release the one they called "King of the Jews."

At this point, one gets the impression this story just might have a happy ending. But that was not to be. The crowd responded to Pilate's offer of freedom for Jesus by shouting "Give us Barabbas!" Jesus was then condemned to death.

We know where this is headed. Under the regular procedures of Roman occupation, executions were not delayed. There was not a higher court of appeal. Our Lord was headed toward suffering and inevitable death.

Between Friday and Sunday morning, remember to read John 18-19. Take note of how events unfolded in a way similar to what happened on that sharp curve in the tracks approaching Santiago de Compostela. From Jesus' arrest in the Garden of Gethsemane on Thursday evening to late Friday afternoon at the place for Roman execution, this was a train wreck in the making. Nothing was going to prevent this disaster. Things were coming off the tracks.

Second, as you read, take note of the demeanor of Jesus. In spite of facing inevitable suffering and death, Jesus was remarkably calm and composed. While this is true in the other gospels, it is even truer in John. The fourth gospel presented Jesus as in such control of his emotions and behavior it was almost as though he was choreographing the events leading to his death. For instance, John insisted that Jesus needed no help to carry his cross. Unlike the other gospels, in John, Simon of Cyrene is not pressed to assist. Jesus carries his own cross. He was in control.

In the synoptic gospels, Jesus prayed that this cup would pass from him. To state that differently, he prayed: "Lord, if it is all the same to you, I would just as soon not suffer and die under these circumstances." In John, Jesus did not even consider the possibility of a reprieve. Instead he expressed his willingness to face what was coming and asked a rhetorical question. "Am I not to drink the cup that the Father has given me?" (18:11).

Jesus had so much self-control that in the gospel of John, he even decided the moment of his death. "When Jesus had received the wine, he said, 'It is finished.' Then he bowed his head and gave up his spirit" (19:30).

More than in the other gospels, John portrayed Jesus as an island of calm resolve in a storm that swirled around him. He was a profile in profound courage even as events went from bad to worse to tragic.

We are not, of course, privy to all the events that led up to Good Friday. On the other hand, there is a certain commonality of human experience over the centuries. For that reason, I think it safe to assume that there was some sort of committee meeting before Jesus and his apostles left on that fateful journey from Judea in the north to the capitol city in the south. Assuming there was such a meeting, Jesus must have said something like, "Fellows, we are going to Jerusalem again. Pack carefully because I cannot promise when or, for that matter, even *if* you will be coming back."

After that, the apostle Thomas, a man known for doubting and questioning, may have thought to himself, "Oh, I don't believe that. We will be back. If anyone asks me where we are going, I will tell them, 'We are going to Jerusalem for the Passover. I expect to have a great time with Jesus and my other friends. I also expect to be back in a couple weeks. In fact, let's plan to meet on the steps of the old synagogue in Capernaum, on the shore of Lake Galilee.' "

As it turned out, that journey was not round-trip. The itinerary was one-way from Judea to Jerusalem to Golgotha and death.

About a hundred years ago, a young Carl Sandburg, the American poet whose work I suspect all of us tasted in high school, if not since, penned a short work on this theme that in spite of what any of us think or claim, death is the destination we have in common. Sandburg wrote:

I am riding on a limited express, one of the crack trains of the nation.
Hurtling across the prairie into blue haze and dark air go fifteen all-steel coaches holding a thousand people.
(All the coaches shall be scrap and rust and all the men and women laughing in the diners and sleepers shall pass to ashes.)

101

I ask a man in the smoker where he is going and he an-
swers: "Omaha."[1]

We might think we are on the way to Omaha or Disney-
land. We might claim we are on the way to riches or success.
In fact, all of us in the diners and sleepers are headed for
ashes to ashes and dust to dust.

For Jesus, the train came off the tracks that Friday. Death
was inevitable. Nothing was going to rescue him. It is a sad
and tragic story. It does not, however, end with suffering and
death. Sunday is coming. Amen.

---

1. Carl Sandburg, *Chicago Poems*, "Limited" (Henry Hold and Company, 1916),
Poem #35, public domain.

Easter Sunday
John 20:1-18

Early on the first day of the week, while it was still dark, Mary Magdalene came to the tomb and saw that the stone had been removed from the tomb. So she ran and went to Simon Peter and the other disciple, the one whom Jesus loved, and said to them, "They have taken the Lord out of the tomb, and we do not know where they have laid him." Then Peter and the other disciple set out and went toward the tomb. The two were running together, but the other disciple outran Peter and reached the tomb first. He bent down to look in and saw the linen wrappings lying there, but he did not go in. Then Simon Peter came, following him, and went into the tomb. He saw the linen wrappings lying there, and the cloth that had been on Jesus' head, not lying with the linen wrappings but rolled up in a place by itself. Then the other disciple, who reached the tomb first, also went in, and he saw and believed; for as yet they did not understand the scripture, that he must rise from the dead. Then the disciples returned to their homes. But Mary stood weeping outside the tomb. As she wept, she bent over to look into the tomb; and she saw two angels in white, sitting where the body of Jesus had been lying, one at the head and the other at the feet. They said to her, "Woman, why are you weeping?" She said to them, "They have taken away my Lord, and I do not know where they have laid him." When she had said this, she turned around and saw Jesus standing there, but she did not know that it was Jesus. Jesus said to her, "Woman, why are you weeping? Whom are you looking for?" Supposing him to be the gardener, she said to him, "Sir, if you have carried him away, tell me where you have laid him, and I will take him away." Jesus said to her, "Mary!" She turned and said to him in Hebrew, "Rabbouni!" (which means Teacher). Jesus said to her, "Do not hold on to me, because I have not yet ascended to the Father. But go to my brothers and say to them, 'I am ascending to my Father and your Father, to my God and your God.' " Mary Magdalene went and announced to the disciples, "I have seen the Lord"; and she told them that he had said these things to her.

BE READY FOR THE POSSIBILITY OF THE RESURRECTION

The last couple of days have been extremely difficult for the followers of Jesus. Thursday, after they had shared a last supper together, the Lord went to the Garden of Gethsemane to pray. There he was arrested by the religious authorities and put on trial in the court of Caiaphas, the high priest. Jesus was charged with blasphemy: false religious teaching. Had Caiaphas heard sufficient evidence to find him guilty, he could have been sentenced to death by stoning.

The high priest was not comfortable with that verdict and turned Jesus over to Pontius Pilate and charged him with the political crime of challenging the governing authority of Rome. Pilate, a political hack of the worst order, tested winds of popular opinion by sticking a wet finger in the air. When a few strident voices shouted "crucify him, crucify him," the Roman governor condemned Jesus to death by crucifixion.

That was a particularly cruel form of execution. Nails were driven through the hands and feet. The full weight of the victim's body was supported only by those iron piercings. After extended suffering from shock, exposure, dehydration, and the loss of blood, death came as a blessed relief. It was not unusual to survive on a cross for days. Jesus, however, was in such a weakened state that he died in the afternoon of the same day he was crucified.

After Roman soldiers were certain of his death, some of his friends took his body down from the cross. They wrapped

Jesus in a linen cloth that contained a hundred pounds of myrrh, aloes, and the other spices. Then they carefully placed Jesus' body in a new tomb in a nearby garden cemetery.

Our gospel reading for this day, John 20:1-18, picks up the narrative at that point. John tells us that early Sunday morning while it was still dark Mary Magdalene went alone to the cemetery. When she arrived, she was stunned to find that the large stone covering the opening to the tomb had been removed. She raced back to where the closest followers of Jesus were staying.

When she arrived, only Simon Peter and an unnamed apostle, described as the "one whom Jesus loved," were up, out of bed, and out in the city streets. Mary Magdalene told them, "They have taken the Lord out of the tomb, and we do not know where they have laid him." This little group of three ran back to the grave. The apostles crawled through the opening into the tomb to investigate. They found the burial clothes, but no body. The gospel writer observed that "as yet they (referring to the apostles) did not understand the scripture, that he must rise from the dead" (v. 9).

When the men left the cemetery, Mary Magdalene remained. As she wept, she bent down, looked into the tomb and saw two angels, dressed in white. The angels inquired as to why she was crying and she responded, "They have taken away my Lord, and I do not know where they have laid him" (v. 13).

Notice what is happening here. Mary Magdalene came to the cemetery intending to grieve the death of Jesus. She was surprised to find an empty tomb and concluded the body of Jesus had been stolen. Even after the apostles discovered the empty burial clothes, Mary Magdalene remained clueless. It did not occur to her that this could be anything but the work of grave robbers. Even the appearance of angels did not get her to stop looking for a dead Jesus.

The story continues that when she came out of the tomb, Jesus was standing there. The Lord spoke to her, "Woman, why are you weeping? Whom are you looking for?" (v. 15). At first, Mary Magdalene still did not get it. She mistook Jesus for one of the cemetery gardeners. She even asked Jesus if he was the one who moved the body. A moment passed before Jesus simply said her name, "Mary."

When she heard her name, she finally recognized Jesus. The tears dried from her eyes. Her spirits were lifted. She began to think clearly. No one had stolen his body because Jesus was no longer dead. Death could not destroy him. The grave could not hold him. He was risen.

With the sound of the risen Christ calling her name still sounding in her ears, Mary Magdalene raced back to tell the other followers of Christ. As she approached, she breathlessly shouted the news, "I have seen the Lord" (v. 18).

It did not all happen that day. It took more time, but eventually the full meaning of what Mary Magdalene reported dawned on Jesus' followers. There was more significance in this than an empty tomb. There was even more to it than Jesus' resurrection way back then. The good news of the gospel is not simply that Jesus lived in first-century Jerusalem. The gospel is that he lives today and we can know him and the power of his resurrection. This is the message of Easter. We can be lifted from troubles to possibilities, from despair to joy, from fear to courage, and from defeat to victory. Our lives are worth living because Jesus indeed lives. This is the significance of Easter. Do not go to bed tonight without giving thought to this great truth.

As central as that message is to the meaning this day, I want us to think together about Mary Magdalene. Particularly I am interested in why she didn't immediately recognize Jesus when she saw him standing outside the tomb. Mary Magdalene was one of Jesus' closest followers. He was no stranger. Why didn't she immediately recognize him?

For that matter, why was she even the slightest bit surprised by the empty tomb? She had heard Jesus predict his resurrection. Was she not paying attention when he said that? Why did she not come to the cemetery anticipating an empty tomb?

As people of faith we claim the resurrection of Jesus the Christ as the greatest event in human history. According to the gospel of John, Mary Magdalene was the first witness to the resurrection. As a good friend and loyal follower of Jesus, should she not have taken one look at the stone rolled away and shouted, "Halleluiah! Christ is risen. He is risen indeed." Why didn't she do that?

There are many complex theological, psychological, and historical hypotheses for why that happened. Let us, however, consider the simple and most obvious explanation. This had been a long, terrifying, miserable weekend for Mary Magdalene. She had watched while her friend and spiritual mentor was brutally killed. She had been there to help transport his dead body to the grave. She may have even had his blood on her hands when they laid him in the tomb. Indeed, it had been a miserable weekend.

Mary Magdalene left before dawn to go to the garden cemetery with her heart overflowing with grief. Her mind must have been a repeating loop of scenes with blood, pain, and suffering. To ask why Mary Magdalene was not thinking about the resurrection is like asking Mary Todd Lincoln, "Well, Mrs. Lincoln, other than that, how was the play?"

When overwhelmed by grief, fear, and terrible memories, there is little room in the psyche to process much of anything else. I think we can safely assume that Mary Magdalene considered her life essentially over. As she stood outside the tomb crying, she must have felt as though never again would she know the deep joy and peace that she had known when she walked the hills of Galilee with Jesus.

I think many of us resonate because we have experienced that same feeling. It is the inner experience of taking a swan dive on to a rock pile of trouble. What Mary was feeling is what we feel when the boss says, "You have done a great job for us, but we are making changes and you are not in our plans. Your job has been eliminated. Here is a little severance pay. Good luck." It is the feeling you have when the note on the refrigerator door reads, "I don't love you anymore. I am leaving. My lawyer will be in touch." It is being at the scene of the accident when the policeman tells you, "We have called the ambulance, but it appears your husband died of his injuries." It is the feeling that overwhelms you when the doctor says, "The lab reports are back. The results are not good. You have a very aggressive form of cancer." That was Mary Magdalene's experience that Sunday morning in the garden cemetery. She felt as though her life had caved in. She was on the verge of being crushed by despair.

Yet Mary did not give up. She kept alive a little spark of hope; a tiny flicker of faith's possibility. In spite of all that weekend's evidence to the contrary, Mary Magdalene remained open to believing that the Creator and sustainer of this world is a God who intends things for good and not for harm; a God who promotes life rather than settling for death. Deep within her heart, Mary never gave up believing that God had not abandoned her and sooner or later, she would see the evidence of God's presence.

Frankly, her faith did not bear fruit easily or quickly. It did not happen when the stone was rolled away or when she realized the grave was empty. She was not impressed by the conversation with angels or by the sight of Jesus standing in the garden. For whatever reason, only when she heard Jesus speak her name did she grasp the significance of what was happening. It was as if a little corner of the drab reality of her life lifted, and Mary Magdalene was able to take a peek at eternity. She reacted by shouting, "I have seen the Lord" and her life was changed.

If she had lost hope and let herself be crushed by despair would Mary Magdalene have even recognized the risen Christ when he called her name? On one hand, I really do not know. One the other hand, I am convinced that Elizabeth Barrett Browning had it right when she wrote,

> *Earth's crammed with heaven,*
> *And every common bush afire with God;*
> *But only he who sees, takes off his shoes,*
> *The rest sit round it and pluck blackberries.*[1]

Indeed, earth is absolutely crammed with evidence of God's presence. However, the only people who even notice the divine within the ordinary are those who are open to the possibility of believing. If you are not willing to look at the world through eyes of faith, you will not likely notice that "every common bush is afire with God." This openness to seeing the possibilities of faith is not easy to maintain. The dark underbelly of living's negative circumstances can close our eyes to faith. Things can and do happen that cause us to despair and even to lose all hope. When that happens, we easily slide into the ranks of those who expend their life's energy merely sitting in a circle plucking blackberries. At best this means living with less joy. At worst, it means standing at the tomb in tears, clueless as to what it means, and wondering how you are going to go on from here.

No matter what the circumstances of your life, don't lose hope. Remain open to the possibility of resurrection; the possibility of new life. You can be lifted from troubles to possibilities, from despair to joy, from fear to courage, from defeat to victory. Hold tight to this possibility: Because he lives you can face tomorrow. You can face your fears. You can even face your own death and be unafraid. Your life is truly worth living because he lives. This is the message of Easter.

---

1. Elizabeth Barrett Browning, *Aurora Leigh*, from Sonnet 86, published in 1856, public domain.

Easter 2
John 20:19-31

When it was evening on that day, the first day of the week, and the doors of the house where the disciples had met were locked for fear of the Jews, Jesus came and stood among them and said, "Peace be with you." After he said this, he showed them his hands and his side. Then the disciples rejoiced when they saw the Lord. Jesus said to them again, "Peace be with you. As the Father has sent me, so I send you." When he had said this, he breathed on them and said to them, "Receive the Holy Spirit. If you forgive the sins of any, they are forgiven them; if you retain the sins of any, they are retained." But Thomas (who was called the Twin), one of the twelve, was not with them when Jesus came. So the other disciples told him, "We have seen the Lord." But he said to them, "Unless I see the mark of the nails in his hands, and put my finger in the mark of the nails and my hand in his side, I will not believe." A week later his disciples were again in the house, and Thomas was with them. Although the doors were shut, Jesus came and stood among them and said, "Peace be with you." Then he said to Thomas, "Put your finger here and see my hands. Reach out your hand and put it in my side. Do not doubt but believe." Thomas answered him, "My Lord and my God!" Jesus said to him, "Have you believed because you have seen me? Blessed are those who have not seen and yet have come to believe." Now Jesus did many other signs in the presence of his disciples, which are not written in this book. But these are written so that you may come to believe that Jesus is the Messiah, the Son of God, and that through believing you may have life in his name.

THE VALUE
OF DOUBT

Is it not interesting the way a nickname can stick to a person? An uncle of mine, now long deceased, was nicknamed "Fat." As a small boy he was grossly overweight and cruel neighborhood children hung that moniker on him. "Hey, who is the big kid out on the playground?" "Oh, that's Fat Casteel."

The puzzling part of the story is that as an adult my uncle was not particularly overweight, yet he retained the nickname. Friends and family always called him Fat. It is curious how a nickname becomes a permanent part of a person's identity.

Something similar happened to Thomas, one of Jesus' apostles. Since biblical times this close follower of our Lord has been known as *Doubting* Thomas. As there were reasons for my uncle to be called Fat, so there were reasons for Thomas to be called Doubting. It had to do with some of the ways that Thomas thought and interacted with others.

In some ways, Dr. Sheldon Cooper shares some personality traits with the apostle Thomas. Played by the actor Jim Parsons, Sheldon Cooper is one of the characters on the popular television program *The Big Bang Theory*. Sheldon is a twenty or thirty-something theoretical physicist with two Ph.D.s. Critics describe this television character as socially awkward because he has almost no interpersonal awareness or skill. Consequently, he is given to saying insensitive

115

things at inappropriate times. However, there is more to it than social awkwardness. Sheldon is a hardcore realist who utters whatever thoughts flit through his mind. When he has a question he can be very direct. As a scientist, he possesses enormous intellectual curiosity and accepts as truth only that which can be verified through the human senses. If Sheldon cannot touch it, smell it, taste it, see it, or hear it, he doesn't believe it. That results in Sheldon having a limited understanding of what is true. To say the least, the Sheldon Cooper character is not given to poetic imagination. He seems not to have the capacity to stand in awe at the evening sunset, to thrill at the sound of a Bach chorale, or to rejoice at the sound of children laughing. Because of this particular characteristic, issues of faith do not come easily to Dr. Sheldon Cooper. Some of those same things might be said of the apostle Thomas, nicknamed the Doubter.

Thomas is mentioned in all four of the gospels. In the first three, Matthew, Mark, and Luke all we get is his name listed among the other apostles and a curious comment about how his name means "twin." The fourth gospel provides more details. These offer flashes of insight into the apostle's ways of thinking and doing.

In John's gospel, Jesus got word from Mary and Martha that Lazarus, their brother and Jesus' friend, was seriously ill. Jesus said to the apostles "Let us go to Judea again" (John 11:7). This band of his closest followers cautioned Jesus. Lazarus lived in Bethany, just a few miles from Jerusalem. Jesus had many enemies there. If they went to Bethany, there was a chance that Jesus would die. When this danger was presented to Jesus, he was unconcerned. He wanted to go to Bethany and see his friends, Mary, Martha, and Lazarus. Thomas spoke up and said: "Let us also go, that we may die with him" (John 11:16).

There are a couple ways to interpret Thomas' comment. It might be an expression of enormous courage. Perhaps, Thomas was not afraid to die and he was simply encouraging the others. "Come on. Let's go to Bethany and support Jesus even if it means we die with him." On the other hand Thomas could be expressing sarcasm. "Let's go to Bethany and die. Now, there is a great idea. Let me suggest that we save the long walk to Bethany. Let's hold hands, sing "Lord, I'm Coming Home" and jump off that cliff over there. Yes, yes, let us go to Bethany, that we might die with him."

Was Thomas offering encouragement or sarcasm? It could be either. Since we do not have access to a video where we can hear the words and see the body language, we cannot know for sure.

Thomas' second cameo came during the dinner table conversation on the night of our Lord's betrayal and arrest. Here we glimpse Thomas' preference for language that is clear and straightforward. He was a "tell it like it is" realist who seemed to have no patience for speaking with rhetorical flourish. In this particular incident Thomas seemed impatient with Jesus because our Lord had not expressed himself as clearly as Thomas wanted.

Jesus had just commented "Do not let your hearts be troubled. Believe in God, believe also in me. In my Father's house there are many dwelling places. If it were not so, would I have told you that I go to prepare a place for you?" (John 14:1-2). Then a verse later Jesus continues, "And you know the way to the place where I am going" (John 14:4).

When Thomas heard this, he was not satisfied. He wanted clarification and asked a follow-up question. "Lord, we do not know where you are going. How can we know the way?" (John 14:5). To embellish and paraphrase a bit, "Jesus, you need to be clearer about this journey. If you want us to show up where you are going, give us a map. Write out the directions. Don't just leave us with lovely words about the Father's house having many dwelling places. Be specific about the way we are supposed to go."

The third appearance of Thomas in John is the most memorable. This is the incident that solidifies his reputation as the doubting one. It is also today's gospel reading.

Early in the morning of this same day, Mary Magdalene had gone to the tomb to mourn the death of Jesus. She was stunned when she found the grave empty. She first assumed that Jesus' body had been stolen. After some initial confusion, she recognized the risen Savior when he spoke to her. Mary Magdalene ran back to the others and reported, "I have seen the Lord."

It was evening. The followers of Jesus still did not know exactly what to make of the day's events. They still feared for their own lives. They were gathered behind a locked door when Jesus came and stood among them. He said, "Peace be with you" (v. 19).

This is no transparent ghost. This is not some figment of their collective imaginations. They recognized the risen Christ as the one with whom they had been traveling the Galilean hills. He showed them the nail holes in his hands and the spear wound in his side. As Jesus did this, he breathed on them and said, "Receive the Holy Spirit" (v. 22). And then he was gone.

Thomas was not with them when this happened. There was no indication where he was. Perhaps he had gone on an errand. Perhaps he really was the most courageous among them and, went off to confront those who plotted to put Jesus to death. All we are told is that he was not present when Jesus appeared among the others.

In time, Thomas returned to the locked room but by then Jesus had gone. The others told him, "We have seen the Lord." Thomas was unimpressed. He said, "Unless I see the mark of nails in his hands, and put my finger in the mark of the nails and my hand in his side, I will not believe" (v. 25). This is the statement that earned him the "Doubting Thomas" nickname. He was either unwilling or, perhaps, even unable to accept something as important as faith in the resurrection purely on the testimony of others. He needed some evidence. "Unless I see the mark of the nails in his hands, and put my finger in the mark of the nails and my hand in his side, I will not believe."

I may be going out on a limb on this, but I think we can be fairly certain that Thomas did not have a sticker on the side of his fishing boat that claimed, "The Bible said it. I believe it. That settles it." In the absence of firsthand, convincing evidence, Thomas asked questions. He wrestled with matters of faith. He doubted.

Far from being critical, I want to commend doubting. Doubt is essential to the maturing of one's faith. Frederick Buechner called doubts "the ants in the pants of faith. They keep it awake and moving."[1] Thomas understood that doubt is what pushes us to grow in our faith. If it was not for the God-given capacities to question, to push for clarification, to doubt, we would never move beyond the untested certainty of childhood.

Think of it this way: Doubt is to faith as a transmission is to an automobile. Let me explain. Think of how as an automobile pulls away from the stop sign, the engine sounds as though it is working harder and harder. In a matter of a few moments, you experience a gentle bump. Even though the car continues to pick up speed, you notice the engine isn't working as hard. It isn't making as much noise. That is because the car's transmission has shifted you into a higher gear. Doubt is like a transmission. It shifts us to a different faith gear; that is, into a more mature faith.

119

It is inevitable that on your faith journey, you will experience times of doubt. When that happens, don't run away. Face your doubts. Deal with them. Struggling with doubt is a faith-building process. Wrestling with doubt has the potential to take you to that place Dostoyevsky described when he said: "I do not believe as a child does; my hosannas have been forged in the crucible of doubt."[2]

There is, of course, an important caveat to consider. As with any good idea, doubt can be taken too far. Doubt has the capacity to move us beyond an immature faith. On the other hand, if we become consumed by doubt we risk sliding into cynicism, believing little or nothing. Our credo then is reduced to nothing more than a list of what we do not believe.

This principle is expressed in the gospel reading for today. A week after the first Easter, the risen Christ returned to the room where the apostles were staying. Jesus stretched out his hands to Thomas and said, in essence, "You said you would not believe until you had an opportunity to see and to touch. You now can see me. Step forward and touch me." Thomas was moved to faith and said, "My Lord and my God." When Thomas saw and touched Jesus, his questions were answered. His doubts were resolved. He believed.

Yet the story does not end there. Jesus said to Thomas, "Have you believed because you have seen me? Blessed are those who have not seen and yet have come to believe" (v. 29). With these words, Jesus was also addressing us. Not a one of us was present when Jesus showed Thomas his hands and side. If we are to have faith, we are going to have to believe without having seen and touched.

The twin dangers of faith are to believe anything because we never have a doubt or to go to the other extreme and never believe anything because our doubts overwhelm us. We need to find a way to live with the tension and the ambiguity between those extremes.

Indeed, doubt is an interesting thing. God's love comes to us and strengthens us to get through those times of doubt and helps us to shift to a more mature understanding of faith. But sometimes in the face of crushing doubt, God's grace comes as the strength to just go ahead and believe; to keep on keeping on until faith begins to grow. To paraphrase John Wesley, sometimes we must live by faith until we have faith.

Thanks be to God who gives us the grace and the strength to do just that.

Amen and amen.

---

1. Frederick Buechner, *Beyond Words: The ABC of Faith*, www.goodreads.com/Buechner quotes.

2. Oft quoted in various forms. Original source probably either Dostoyevsky's personal notebook or his letters.

Easter 3
John 21:1-19

After these things Jesus showed himself again to the disciples by the Sea of Tiberias; and he showed himself in this way. Gathered there together were Simon Peter, Thomas called the Twin, Nathanael of Cana in Galilee, the sons of Zebedee, and two others of his disciples. Simon Peter said to them, "I am going fishing." They said to him, "We will go with you." They went out and got into the boat, but that night they caught nothing. Just after daybreak, Jesus stood on the beach; but the disciples did not know that it was Jesus. Jesus said to them, "Children, you have no fish, have you?" They answered him, "No." He said to them, "Cast the net to the right side of the boat, and you will find some." So they cast it, and now they were not able to haul it in because there were so many fish. That disciple whom Jesus loved said to Peter, "It is the Lord!" When Simon Peter heard that it was the Lord, he put on some clothes, for he was naked, and jumped into the sea. But the other disciples came in the boat, dragging the net full of fish, for they were not far from the land, only about a hundred yards off. When they had gone ashore, they saw a charcoal fire there, with fish on it, and bread. Jesus said to them, "Bring some of the fish that you have just caught." So Simon Peter went aboard and hauled the net ashore, full of large fish, a hundred fifty-three of them; and though there were so many, the net was not torn. Jesus said to them, "Come and have breakfast." Now none of the disciples dared to ask him, "Who are you?" because they knew it was the Lord. Jesus came and took the bread and gave it to them, and did the same with the fish. This was now the third time that Jesus appeared to the disciples after he was raised from the dead. When they had finished breakfast, Jesus said to Simon Peter, "Simon son of John, do you love me more than these?" He said to him, "Yes, Lord; you know that I love you." Jesus said to him, "Feed my lambs." A second time he said to him, "Simon son of John, do you love me?" He said to him, "Yes, Lord; you know that I love you." Jesus said to him, "Tend my sheep." He said to him the third time, "Simon son of John, do you love me?" Peter felt hurt because he said to him the third time, "Do you love me?" And he said to him, "Lord, you know everything; you know that I love you." Jesus said to him, "Feed my sheep. Very truly, I tell you, when you were younger, you used to fasten your own belt and to go wherever you wished. But when you grow old, you will stretch out your hands, and someone else will fasten a belt around you and take you where you do not wish to go." (He said this to indicate the kind of death by which he would glorify God.) After this he said to him, "Follow me."

The Awesome Power of FUD

It happened many years ago, but I remember the experience as if it was yesterday. It was late September and I was in the first grade. The teacher assigned an art project. "Draw a picture of a boat. Do your very best," she instructed.

I was excited. I specialized in drawing boats, particularly the ships of the United States Navy. My mother always praised my boat pictures.

With the precision ordinarily reserved for the drafting tables of the shipyard at Norfolk, Virginia, I crafted what I believed was a perfectly scaled drawing of a U.S. Navy battleship. The pictures with which I was familiar showed battleship decks lined with waving sailors, I decided to do the same. That added touch, I concluded would certainly result in extra credit for my art project.

Before returning our artwork, the teacher took the opportunity to give a lesson. I do not recall everything she said that day. I do, however, distinctly recall that she held up my drawing as an illustration of how *not* to draw a boat. "This child," she patiently explained, "only used one color. He drew the entire boat in black crayon. I am not certain what all these lines are on the deck. I suppose they are people, but I cannot really tell."

Part of me wanted to jump to my feet and explain that, of course, the ship was black crayon on white paper. Every photograph of a ship that I had ever seen was in black and white. At our house, we did not subscribe to magazines with color photographs. And yes, those lines were people. I admit they were not very good people, but I was only six years old. I got tired of drawing stick figures, so I just used lines.

As much as I wanted to defend myself, I didn't. I was too overwhelmed by the teacher's criticism. On that day, I decided to give up drawing boats. In fact, I decided never again to submit my drawings to public scrutiny.

Please don't misunderstand. I do not blame the teacher. She was young and inexperienced. Obviously she needed more teacher college lessons on being sensitive to the feelings of children. On the other hand, she was an outstanding judge of children's art. She saw immediately what I was to confirm over the years. I have no gift for drawing boats. Most of all, however, I remember that day as the one in which I was introduced to the awesome power of FUD.

You may not be familiar with the expression, but I suspect nearly everyone has had the experience. The term FUD was first used in the 1920s to refer to a common sales technique. When the customer was thinking about buying your competitor's product, destroy the customer's confidence in the competition by applying the awesome power of fear, uncertainty, and doubt. "That company does not service what they sell." "That is a new company. They don't have the experience we have." "That is an old company. They are stuck in the past." FUD is the sales term for tearing down the competition by introducing the awesome power of fear, uncertainty, and doubt.

Of course, FUD is experienced in more settings than widget sales. For instance, talk radio is little more than a bountiful application of fear, uncertainty, and doubt to current events. The success of negative political advertisement is largely due to the power of FUD. By introducing fear, uncertainty, and doubt, the electorate's confidence in a candidate is undermined. There are work places where spreading FUD has been raised to an art form. Some marriages seem committed to destroying one's significant other by the liberal application of FUD. Some parents never miss an opportunity to undermine the self-confidence of their children by finding ways to make them doubt their possibilities. When important people in our lives die, fear and uncertainty about the future are commonly experienced.

I experienced FUD in a first grade art lesson on boat drawing. In the twinkling of an eye, I went from a self-confident little boy to a quivering mass of devastated protoplasm. Such is the power of FUD. It happens. There is nothing rare about the experience of fear, uncertainty, and doubt. These voracious destroyers of confident living linger at the edge of life, waiting for an opportunity to rush in and take charge.

The image that comes to mind is the crab pot in a fish market. These don't need lids because any crab trying to escape is always pulled back in by the others. As Michael Corleone puts it in *Godfather III*, "Just when I thought I was out... they pulled me back in." That can and does happen. When we least expect it, some person or experience can grab hold with claws of fear, uncertainty, and self-doubt. As people of faith, our challenge is to find a way to live confidently and victoriously in a world where the awesome power of FUD is an ever-present possibility.

The gospel lesson for today comes from the first nineteen verses of the final chapter of the book of John. I submit that this story both portrays the power of FUD and offers some guidance on how to deal with it.

The setting was after the crucifixion and resurrection of Jesus and seven of the apostles were fishing on the Sea of Galilee. Think about that for a moment. That was the job they had before they met Jesus. They had already encountered the risen Christ. Jesus had already charged them saying, "As the

127

Father has sent me, so I send you." The Christ had already breathed on them the power of the Holy Spirit. He had already empowered them to forgive the sins of others (John 20:21-22).

The world awaited the good news of the gospel of Jesus Christ and they were charged with spreading the word. They had been called to change the world. One would have thought that they would be excited to get started on this new ministry. They were not, however, "chomping at the bit" to get going. Simon Peter said, "I am going fishing" and six other apostles joined him.

Why did they do that? There must be some fear, uncertainty, and doubt at work. "How can we continue without Jesus? He was our leader. We are just common hill folk from Galilee. Nobody is going to listen to us. How can we preach to the world? We have trouble putting a sentence together."

Perchance the full text of what Simon Peter said that day was, "Come on, fellas. I am going fishing. At least we know how to do that. Any of you want to go with me?" And so, about sundown, seven apostles got into a boat, pushed off from shore, spent the entire night fishing, and did not catch a single fish. I am sure that failure only deepened their spiritual crisis. "We are failures at fishing for fish, how can we succeed at fishing for the children of God?"

Just as dawn was breaking, a stranger called to them from the shore. "Cast the net to the right side of the boat, and you will find some" (v. 6). As a group of professional fishermen, it must have seemed a silly suggestion to try the other side of their narrow boat, but they did it anyway.

As they struggled with the weight of a net of fish, one of the apostles recognized that the stranger was really Jesus. That apostle told Peter and Peter swam to shore. The remaining fishermen struggled to beach the overweight boat. When they arrived, they found Jesus cooking breakfast.

Let's step back a little and assess what was happening. The opening of the story portrayed symptoms of FUD. Their little group was so discombobulated by the events of the past several weeks that several went back to being fishermen; only to discover that they could not even do that very well. Then Jesus appeared to them and provided guidance for getting through times of FUD. That guidance is what I would call the ABCs of getting through times of fear, uncertainty, and doubt. Let's look at this.

A: When under the influence of FUD learn the overall lesson from John 21. Get some perspective. People were dealing with fear, uncertainty, and doubt in the first century. They got through it and so can we. When zapped by the power of FUD, refuse to slide into the despair of "oh woe is me — nobody knows the misery I know." FUD has been and remains a common human experience. Over the centuries, multitudes have experienced failure at fishing and first grade boat drawing. Fear from being threatened, uncertainty about our future, and crippling self-doubt are common to the human experience. When we keep that reality in mind, the experience of FUD becomes more manageable.

B: Accept that getting through FUD requires trusting God and stepping out in faith. Notice that the apostles did not recognize Jesus standing on the shore. He was a stranger when he called, "Throw the net on the other side of the boat."

That suggestion must not have made much sense. These were professional fishermen. They must have already tried the other side of the boat. They did not, however, argue the point. They just did it and they discovered it worked.

There is much about our faith that doesn't necessarily seem reasonable. Things like love your enemies; instead of revenge, do good to those who hate you; understand that the last shall be first; if offended, turn the other cheek. These things do not seem reasonable, but like putting the net on the other side of the boat, they work. Trust God. Trust the teachings of the faith. Step out in faith and keep on keeping on.

C: Remember that tomorrow is coming. The apostles fished all night and didn't catch a thing. Then came the dawn and everything changed. What a wonderful reminder that life comes to us in daily segments. Today may be the absolute worst day of your life, but tomorrow is coming.

A friend of mine loves to preach an Easter sermon in which he reminds the congregation of an important lesson from resurrection weekend. When all seems lost, just "wait three days." When faced with great difficulty, don't panic; don't despair, don't lose hope, just wait a few days. Perhaps with the dawn of a new day you will be given strength when today all you feel is weakness. Perhaps with a new day you will find resolution to what seems impossible today. Eventually the agony of today will succumb to inexorable passage of time. Tomorrow is always coming and with it will come new possibilities. Hang on to that great truth.

I wish I could tell you that the awesome power of FUD can be avoided or at least easily defeated. That is not true. We live as imperfect people in an imperfect world. Therefore, the promise of our faith is not to avoid fear, uncertainty, and doubt. The promise of our faith is that we can live confidently and victoriously when the possibility of FUD lingers at the edge of life.

Keep the threat in perspective. Trust God and step out in faith. Never lose hope in what tomorrow will bring. Most of all, believe not only that Jesus was alive back then, but he lives today. The power of the risen Christ is still set free. We can connect with that power and be strengthened by it. Because he lives, we can face tomorrow and be unafraid. Our fears can be conquered. Our uncertainties and self-doubt can be handled. That is the great promise of our faith.

Thanks be to God for that. Amen and Amen.

Easter 4
John 10:22-30

At that time the festival of the Dedication took place in Jerusalem. It was winter, and Jesus was walking in the temple, in the portico of Solomon. So the Jews gathered around him and said to him, "How long will you keep us in suspense? If you are the Messiah, tell us plainly." Jesus answered, "I have told you, and you do not believe. The works that I do in my Father's name testify to me; but you do not believe, because you do not belong to my sheep. My sheep hear my voice. I know them, and they follow me. I give them eternal life, and they will never perish. No one will snatch them out of my hand. What my Father has given me is greater than all else, and no one can snatch it out of the Father's hand. The Father and I are one."

ON WELCOMING
THE IMPERFECT

Our gospel lesson for the day opens with John telling us it is time for the Festival of Dedication. Over the centuries, this festival has evolved into what we know as Hanukah. It commemorates events that occurred about a century and a half before the birth of Christ. Since Hanukah is usually in November or December some Christians mistakenly think of it as Jewish Christmas. It is not. If anything, the meaning of Hanukah comes closer to the Fourth of July than to Christmas. Both celebrate revolutions that resulted in setting people free from an oppressive outsider.

Briefly, here is the story.[1] About three and a half centuries before Jesus was born, Alexander the Great came to rule Judea. Unlike some rulers, Alexander wanted more than taxes from those he conquered. He wanted to change the culture, the religion, the language, and the hearts of the people as well as to collect heavy taxes. Toward that end, Alexander the Great pushed for Greek ways of worshiping, speaking, thinking, and doing.

Over the next couple centuries, by way of that inexorable osmosis that comes with the passing of time, Greek ways seeped into and began to replace Jewish ways. The distinctiveness of the Jewish people was being lost. Things came to a head in 167 BCE when Antiochus IV, the one currently in the line of Alexander the Great, appointed his own person to be the high priest. Whereas the Jews believed the high priest should be called by God, Antiochus IV considered the job just another political appointment. Antiochus put his own man in office and then, among other things, began to require that pigs be sacrificed on the high altar.

This insult was more than any self-respecting Jew could tolerate. It was one thing to wear Greek fashions or to conduct business in the Greek language, but it was quite another to desecrate the holiest place in Jewish life with the blood of swine. Faithful Jews were outraged. Led by the family of the legitimate high priest, a revolution erupted. Eventually what was called the Maccabean revolt was triumphant. The Jews drove the occupiers from their temple and their country. The Jewish people rejoiced because their God Yahweh had once again delivered them from their enemies.

The faithful then began to purge Greek influence from their community life and faith practices. At the top of the priority list was the ritual purification of the temple. That required first lighting the eternal flame representing the presence of God in the temple. Unfortunately, this posed a problem. The supply of special oil for the eternal flame was nearly exhausted. In fact, they could find only oil enough for a single day and it took eight days to purify a new supply. By faith, they immediately lit the lamp and started the eight day purification process. They were confident that the God who delivered them from the Greeks would sustain the eternal flame until the oil supply could be replenished.

According to the legend, that is exactly what happened. The oil for a single day burned for eight days. Exactly how and why a one day supply of oil lasted for eight days, I do not know. It is a mystery.

The lessons of Hanukah are many. Beware of Greeks bearing the gift of their ways of thinking and doing. Remember that impure pagans can lead you astray. Outsiders can take over your country, undermine your culture, and destroy your religion. Stay pure. Hang tight to your way of life. These are all incredibly important lessons.

It is, however, also important to remember this caveat. What happened in 167 BCE cannot be applied as a template for every era and circumstance. That caveat is at the heart of today's gospel reading. The Romans were occupying Jerusalem, not the Greeks. The Romans were more interested in political control and tax collecting than desecrating the temple by sacrificing pigs. However, Judeans had learned the importance of vigilance. Jewish faith practices must never again be mocked. By the time of Jesus, the Pharisees, not the Maccabees, were the ones in charge of keeping Jewish faith practices pure.

John told us that Jesus was walking in the temple. The scripture mentions it was winter. This insertion of a weather report might simply indicate it was a particularly cold day. On the other hand, maybe when John said, "It was winter" (v. 22), he was referring to the icy attitude of those Pharisees who approached Jesus. Those were the first-century religion police. They always had an agenda. One bent close enough to Jesus that the master caught a whiff of moldy breath and rudely asked, "How long will you keep us in suspense? If you are the Messiah, tell us plainly." Jesus answered, "I have told you, and you do not believe. The works that I do in my Father's name testify to me"… "My sheep hear my voice. I know them, and they follow me"… "No one will snatch them out of my hand"… "The Father and I are one" (vv. 24b-25, 27-28, 30).

Let me suggest a way to understand this interchange. I don't think the Pharisees really wanted to know "if" Jesus was the messiah. Jesus had already answered that question. They wanted to know what type of messiah he planned to be. Was Jesus going to be in the mold of Judah Maccabee? Did Jesus plan to drive out the Romans the way Judah Maccabee drove out the Greeks? Did he support the Pharisees and the religion police in their efforts to purge society of every religiously impure person and negative influence? If that was Jesus' objective, the Pharisees just might support him. Their concern was that Jesus had not shown much interest in purging impurity. He had drawn his closest followers from the lowest ranks of ordinary people. He associated with tax collectors and Gentiles. He treated women as valued children of God. He failed to condemn the Romans with sufficient enthusiasm. He seemed not to care one whit about keeping sabbath rules. They wanted a Messiah committed to purging impurity. The Pharisees remembered what they had learned from Antiochus IV and the desecration of the temple.

To paraphrase Jesus' response: "Hey fellows, I just preach and people respond. Like sheep respond to the voice of the shepherd, they hear my voice and come. Rather than judging, I welcome people as children of a loving God and I base that welcome simply on the fact they come." Jesus did not exclude those the Pharisees deemed impure.

Jesus continued by saying, "The Father and I are one." In this context, I take that to mean, "God and I are on the same page on this matter." A couple of chapters later, John remembered Jesus saying, "And I, when I am lifted up from the earth, I will draw *all* people to myself" (John 12:32, emphasis mine).

Notice the critical difference between the approach of the Pharisees and the approach of Jesus. The Pharisees wanted to emphasize purging the impure. Jesus wanted to emphasize reaching out and even welcoming the imperfect. As the American poet, Edwin Markham put it in his little verse, "Outwitted."

He drew a circle that shut me out —
Heretic, a rebel, a thing to flout.
But love and I had the wit to win:
We drew a circle and took him In![2]

The Pharisees wanted to draw the circle to shut some out. They wanted to say, "You and you and you are all right — but you can't come." Jesus, on the other hand, wanted to draw the circle to include all people. Jesus was a "y'all come" sort of fellow.

There is said to be a local congregation so committed to the core value of hospitality that they include the following in their Sunday bulletin each week.

Welcome to this church. We welcome those who are single, married, divorced, gay, filthy rich, dirt poor, "o no habla inglés." We offer a special welcome to the crying newborn, to those skinny as a rail, as well as to those who could afford to lose a few pounds.

We will welcome you if you can sing like an angel, but we will also welcome you if you can't carry a note in a bucket. You're welcome here if you're "just browsing," just woke up, or just got out of jail. To those who can claim they were an "Every Sunday Attender" where they used to live and to those who seldom darken the door of any church, we say, "Come on in."

You are welcome here if you are a teenager growing up too fast or if you over seventy and never grew up. We welcome soccer moms, NASCAR dads, starving artists, tree-huggers, latte-sippers, vegetarians, and junk-food eaters.

We welcome those who are in recovery or still addicted. We are especially equipped here at this church to welcome you if you are "down in the dumps" or having some sort of life crisis. In this congregation you can probably find at least one person able to identify with your struggle — purely from personal experience.

If you happen to be one of those folks who just does not like "organized religion," you will love this church. This congregation has raised being "unorganized" to an art form.

We offer a special welcome to those who think the earth is flat, work too hard, are looking for work, or never intend to find a job. We will welcome you even if you just blew your last paycheck at the casino.

We will welcome you if can't spell or have illegible handwriting. We welcome those who are inked, pierced, or both. We will even welcome you if your tattoos are illegible or have misspellings. Perhaps you came to church this morning because grandma is visiting. She wanted to go to church and she needed a ride. Welcome. If you got lost in traffic and wound up here by mistake, welcome.

We especially welcome those who could use a prayer right now or those who had religion shoved down their throats as kids. We welcome tourists, seekers, doubters and bleeding hearts, but we especially welcome you![3]

I suspect if we gave it a little thought, we might be able to add a few more categories to that congregation's list of who is welcome. On the other hand, the obvious questions need asked. What about the important lessons learned during the reign of Antiochus IV? If we are not careful about who we welcome, isn't there a danger that the next thing we know someone will want to start sacrificing pigs on the communion table? Won't we create a problem by incorporating too much diversity?

In "Outwitted," Edwin Markham seems pretty smug in responding to those who draw a circle to keep some people out. Those who exclude others behave like first-century Pharisees that are not all that certain they even want to include Jesus in their group. On the other hand, the Pharisees make a valid point. Is it not risky to be inclusive? In fact, can it not be downright disruptive and even dangerous to be inclusive? I am sensitive to those who raise these kinds of questions. Unregulated, rampant inclusivity is risky.

And yet, the scripture teaches us that we are all children of the same parent God and we are called to love one another. By faith we are called to be on the side of drawing circles to include rather than to exclude.

Exactly how that works, I must confess, I don't fully understand. On the other hand, I don't understand how a one day supply of oil burned for eight days. It is just one of those wondrous things. Some folks call those amazing happenings the miracles of a loving, faithful God.

Brothers and sisters, y'all come. We are all the children of God. Amen and amen.

---

1. There are elements of the story of Hanukah that would not have been part of understanding the Festival of Dedication in the first century. For instance, the gospel writer would not have been familiar with the detail about a one day supply of oil burning for seven days. That part of the story is a contribution from the Talmud written several hundred years later. This detail is included because it enriches the story without detracting from the meaning of John 10:22-30.

2. Excerpted from Edwin Markham's poem, "Outwitted," public domain.

3. This is taken from an internet posting that was making the rounds in late 2013. The source has been lost in cyberspace. It has been edited.

Easter 5
John 13:31-35

When he had gone out, Jesus said, "Now the Son of Man has been glorified, and God has been glorified in him. If God has been glorified in him, God will also glorify him in himself and will glorify him at once. Little children, I am with you only a little longer. You will look for me; and as I said to the Jews so now I say to you, 'Where I am going, you cannot come.' I give you a new commandment, that you love one another. Just as I have loved you, you also should love one another. By this everyone will know that you are my disciples, if you have love for one another."

KNOWN BY OUR LOVE

Jesus and the apostles were celebrating that last supper together. Because Jesus was aware Judas was going to betray him, the Lord confronted him. It is an especially uncomfortable conversation that Jesus concluded by telling Judas, "Do quickly what you must do" (13:27).

After the apostle of betrayal slithered out of the room, Jesus turned his attention to those who remained. After a few preliminary remarks, Jesus delivered one of his more familiar teachings. "I give you a new commandment, that you love one another. Just as I have loved you, you also should love one another. By this everyone will know that you are my disciples, if you will have love for one another" (vv. 34-35).

It is often pointed out that the command to love one another, in and of itself, was not a new teaching. It had been a part of Jewish tradition for centuries. In explanatory comments on the Ten Commandments, Deuteronomy 6:5 says, "You shall love the Lord your God with all your heart, and with all your soul and with all your might." Leviticus 19:18 adds that "you should love your neighbor as yourself." The call to love one another was not new to Jewish teaching and it was also present in the wider Greco-Roman world.

We cannot make a case that loving one another was a new idea; at least not in the sense that it was the first time anyone heard about it. On the other hand, it seems plausible to say the newness of which Jesus spoke was that by our love for one another we will be identified as followers of Christ to the wider world. As the church camp song puts it, "They will know we are Christians by our love."

The early church took this new command of Jesus quite seriously and quickly gained the reputation for caring for the needs of one another. Outsiders noticed that particularly in times of plagues and pestilence, Christians did not abandon their sick as was commonplace in that era.[1] Caring for the sick and dying had translated into religious obligation. Outsiders noticed that by loving one another, people's lives were transformed; that those who were loved reciprocated that love; that those identified as followers of Christ committed themselves to building a better world. For instance, Christian faith communities began to found hospitals, orphanages, and schools. As Tertullian, an early church leader reported, the Romans noticed how Christian behavior was out of the ordinary and they frequently exclaimed, "See how they love one another."

It is good to be reminded of this truth. It is easy to forget that we will be known as followers of Christ by our love and not for some other behavior. Of course, every person who has claimed Christ through the ages has not necessarily lived up to the standard of "see how they love one another."

General Leonidas Polk was a corps commander in the Confederate Army of Tennessee. He had the additional duty of being the Episcopal Bishop of Louisiana. Polk was considered a pious, righteous, and sometimes even a self-righteous Christian. Prior to the Battle of Perryville, Kentucky, one of Polk's subordinates, General Benjamin Cheatham encouraged the troops by shouting, "Give 'em hell, boys." A legend persists that the Very Reverend Bishop General Leonidas Polk seconded those encouraging words by saying, "Give it to 'em boys; give 'em what General Cheatham says."[2]

There were 7,621 casualties at Perryville. Thousands of the children of God in both Union and Confederate armies lost their lives in that conflict. There is, of course, something positive to say about Christian military commander refraining from coarse language. However, Jesus instructed us to be known for our love. To my knowledge, he did not encourage us to kill our enemies while refusing to cuss.

In that same way, Jesus did not say that the faithful will be known by the fact we have read the Bible from cover to cover or that we believe everything in the Bible from Genesis right on through the maps. Jesus did not say that they will know us by our ability to recite the Apostles' Creed both forward and backward. Our Lord did not say they will know us by the way we go to church regularly, because we have the outline of a fish on the bumper of our car, or because we claim to believe all the approved doctrines of twenty-first-century cultural Christianity. Jesus said his followers were to be identified by their love for one another.

Yet exactly what does this love for one another look like? How do we know it when we *see* it? How do we know it when we *experience* it? How do we know it when we *do* it?

Let me suggest that the psychologist Harry Stack Sullivan's definition of the state of love provides a nice opening wedge into these questions. To paraphrase ever so slightly, Stack says that whenever you are as concerned about the safety, the satisfaction, or the happiness of another person as you are about your own safety, satisfaction, and happiness, there the state of love exists.

Love is much more than a feeling. It is even more than just about us. The focus of love is to be in our commitment to act in ways that promote the welfare, security, and happiness of others as much as we promote our own welfare, security, and happiness. When this standard of our love is being reciprocated, then we love one another. That understanding dwells at the heart of Jesus' teaching on the expectation that a faithful person will "love our neighbors as ourselves."

The Christian manual of specifics on how to do this is scattered throughout the New Testament. Let me point out a few examples:

• 1 Corinthians 13:4-7 offers some behavioral specifics: "Love is patient; love is kind; love is not envious or boastful or arrogant or rude. It does not insist on its own way; it is not irritable or resentful; it does not rejoice in wrongdoing, but rejoices in the truth. It bears all things, believes all things, hopes all things, endures all things."

• Philippians 2:3 points to overall attitude and motivation. "Do nothing from selfish ambition or conceit, but in humility regard others as better than yourselves."

• Romans 12:9-10: "Let love be genuine; hate what is evil, hold fast to what it good; love one another with mutual affection; outdo one another in showing honor."

• 1 Peter 4:8: "Above all, maintain constant love for one another, for love covers a multitude of sins."

• Galatians 6:10: "So then, whenever we have an opportunity, let us work for the good of all, and especially for those of the family of faith."

Notice that the call to love another is more than loving our friends and our close relatives. The call to faithfulness even requires loving more than our brothers and sisters in Christ. In Luke's gospel, Jesus was quizzed about what one must do to inherit eternal life. He cited the command to love your neighbor as yourself. The questioner followed up with "And who is my neighbor?" In response, Jesus told a parable about how an outsider, a Samaritan acted in loving ways toward the beaten man and thus qualified as a loving neighbor. By the standards of today's lectionary gospel reading, the Samaritan outsider would also be identified as a follower of Jesus Christ because he acted lovingly toward the beaten man at the side of the road. In Matthew, Jesus pushed the circle even wider when he said, "You have heard that it was said, 'You shall love your neighbor and hate your enemy.' But I say to you, love your enemies and pray for those who persecute you" (Matthew 5:43-44). In that passage I just mentioned from Galatians 6, Paul pushed the limits of loving one another to the absolute maximum when he called us to "work for the good of all."

The reason for this is that as human beings, we are inextricably connected to one another. By that I mean we are all children of the same parent God and that puts us all in one family. This oneness we share as children of God forms a worldwide web of connectivity.

In the year 1624, English clergyman, poet, essayist, and lawyer John Donne was pondering this reality. Specifically, Donne was meditating on the question of why an outsider might be concerned about the death of a stranger. His insight is simple, clear, and as relevant today as it was nearly four centuries ago.[3] We mourn because,

No one is an island,
Entire of itself,
Each of us is a piece of the continent,
A part of the main.
If a clod be washed away by the sea,
Europe is the less.
As well as if a promontory were.
As well as if the home of your friend
Or even your own home was washed away.
Each person's death diminishes me,
For I am involved in humankind,
Therefore, do not send a neighbor to find out
For whom the death bell rings.
It rings for you.

We are all kinfolk. Because we are all part of this family of God, we are called to love one another. That means we are called to strive to be as concerned for the safety, satisfaction, and happiness of others as we are concerned for our own safety, satisfaction, and happiness.

Justin Martyr, a second-century theologian and interpreter of the faith, once remarked on how loving one another made a profound difference in the Christian community: "We who used to value the acquisition of wealth and possessions more than anything else now bring what we have into a common fund and share it with anyone who needs it. We used to hate and destroy one another and refused to associate with people of another race or culture. Now, because of Christ, we live together with such people and pray for our enemies."

A love that is as concerned for others as it is concerned for self is the most powerful force in the world. As an unknown poet puts it:

Love changes everything it touches:
It makes heavy burdens light,
Long hours short.
Ordinary faces beautiful,
Houses into homes,
Picnics into banquets,
Wilted daisies into bouquets,
God into sacrifice and sinners into saints.
The poet ends with a challenging query.
Doesn't it make you wonder what might happen to you
If you yielded to God's love?
(source unknown)

Love has the potential to change everything. Experiencing love in your life can change you. Loving another person can change that person. Even you loving another person can change you. In fact, even loving your enemy just might transform that enemy to a friend.

In Christ, we are not only called to love one another, we are to be identified as followers of Jesus Christ by our love.

Thanks be to God for the blessing that comes with loving one another. Amen and amen.

---

1. William McNeill, *Plagues and People* (Garden City, New York: Anchor Books, 1976), p. 108.

2. James McDonough, *James Lee, Chattanooga — A Death Grip on the Confederacy* (Knoxville: University of Tennessee Press, 1984), pp. 243-245.

3. John Donne, "No man is an island, from Meditations for Emergent Occasions, 1624" (with a slight paraphrase to update the language), in public domain.

Easter 6
John 14:23-29

Jesus answered him, "Those who love me will keep my word, and my Father will love them, and we will come to them and make our home with them. Whoever does not love me does not keep my words; and the word that you hear is not mine, but is from the Father who sent me. I have said these things to you while I am still with you. But the Advocate, the Holy Spirit, whom the Father will send in my name, will teach you everything, and remind you of all that I have said to you. Peace I leave with you; my peace I give to you. I do not give to you as the world gives. Do not let your hearts be troubled, and do not let them be afraid. You heard me say to you, 'I am going away, and I am coming to you.' If you loved me, you would rejoice that I am going to the Father, because the Father is greater than I. And now I have told you this before it occurs, so that when it does occur, you may believe."

CAN I GET SOME
HELP OVER HERE?

It is not an uncommon scene. A couple of young men found their way into the weight room at the local exercise facility. They were, perhaps, thirteen or fourteen years of age; just beginning to approach manhood; each day the sweetness of self-confidence grows within them.

At first they lingered at the edge of the weight room admiring that small group that inhabits every work-out facility. These fellows are usually in their twenties or thirties. Their bodies have been sculpted by thousands of hours of strenuous, physical training. Their physiques more resemble super heroes than ordinary human beings. The two young visitors watched while, with seeming ease, one of the body builders did repetitions with a steel bar that actually bent slightly under a weight approaching that of a small pony.

The young men at the edge of the room were intrigued. "I'll bet you I can lift that much," one boasted. "I'll bet I can too," the other retorted. Then they agreed. "Let's try it." When the bench became available, they rushed over. Just to be safe they took one large plate off each end of the steel bar. Unfortunately, they have had no experience with the reality of even the remaining weight.

One of the young men reclined on the bench, pushed his arms upward. With great effort, he managed to roll the bar with its heavy steel weights from the stand that had been holding it. He lowered it to his chest and discovered he didn't have the strength to push it back up. The weight was crushing his chest. His friend struggled to give assistance, but the bar was too heavy for both of them. The fellow on the bottom was in big trouble. He could barely breathe.

After brief moments of struggle, the panicked friend called out, "Can I get some help over here?" Inevitably, one of the super hero types came to the rescue. They have been through this before. In fact, not only have they heard other first time visitors call for help, they have on occasion called for help themselves.

That scenario has familiar counterparts. In fact, most of us know at least a little something about needing help because we have gotten beyond our comfort zone. We are familiar with the plea. "Can I get some help over here?"

It was little Billy Johnson's first day of kindergarten. Understandably, he was frightened. In his brief life, Billy had seldom been dropped off with a room full of total strangers. His mother had tried to prepare him. In fact, she thought she had done everything humanly possible to ready him for his first day of school. However, as she walked down the sidewalk toward her car, Mrs. Johnson looked back toward the kindergarten classroom. There she saw her beloved only child standing on a table in front of the window with his arms outstretched, his terrified face pressed tightly against the glass screaming. "Hey Mom, can I get some help over here?"

Colleen was seventeen years old. She has had a driver's license for about a year. For the most part, she was a very safe, careful driver. Of course, she doesn't know everything she needs to know about operating an automobile. One Saturday afternoon as she returned from a delightful shopping trip to the mall, she ran out of gas about two blocks from home. This had never happened before. She didn't even know what it meant when the car started sputtering, jerking, and gasping. When the engine died, she tried to start it again. When that failed, she abandoned the car and walked home. When she came through the front door, she called out, "Hey Dad, can I get some help over here?"

Unfortunately, feeling the need for a little help can involve issues far more serious than a stalled car or the first day of school. Christine and her husband Dan were returning from an appointment with her physician. Two years ago, Christine was treated for cancer. They assumed this visit would be routine and that the doctor was going to confirm her healthy status. Instead they learned the cancer had metastasized to Christine's liver and lungs. In one doctor's visit, Christine had gone from "cancer survivor" to "cancer warrior." Intensifying the throat-clogging worry was the realization that when they get home, Christine and Dan would need to be prepared to help their not-quite-teenage children deal with the news that their family's future is not as certain as it seemed yesterday. The plea is unavoidable. "Can we get some help over here?"

These experiences are not new to this modern age. Today's lectionary gospel reading comes from a portion of what scholars call Jesus' farewell discourse. It was the evening of Jesus' betrayal, arrest, and trial. The master and his little band of followers were still in the upper room celebrating their last supper together. Jesus had been telling them in as many different ways as possible, "I am going to be betrayed and then killed. I will be leaving you. Tonight is the night. You must be prepared for this" (vv. 23-27).

When you read the farewell discourse with an open mind and an open heart, you sense a palpable anxiety spreading through Jesus' followers. "You are going to leave us alone? How will we get along without you? Hey, Jesus, we are going to need some help over here."

As we might anticipate, Jesus responded with guidance on how to get along when he was not there to direct their every decision; not there to intervene each time they get into trouble. As Mary Hinkle Shore explains, during his farewell discourse, "Jesus tried to show them two elements of reality that were difficult to hold together: He was going away, yet he would not leave them alone."[1]

Little Billy Johnson's mother was faced with that difficult task when she saw her terrified son wailing at the kindergarten classroom window. Mrs. Johnson handled it by stopping on the school sidewalk and turning toward her child. She stood there for a couple minutes so that Billy might be reassured by her ongoing nearness. Then she whispered in a way he might read her lips. "Billy, I must go now, but I will come back. You will be all right. I love you."

Jesus gave his followers that assurance. "I will not leave you orphaned; I am coming to you" (14:18). In the next few verses, Jesus told his followers that even though the world would not see him, they would sense he was near to them. When they cry out, "Can we get some help over here?" his holy presence would be palpable. They will feel his ongoing, unbroken love in their midst.

Of course, there is more to it than that. I am sure little Billy Johnson appreciated seeing his mother standing on the sidewalk but if he was going to deal with the ongoing, terrifying realities of growing up, there were simply some things Billy had to learn.

Jesus touched on this principle in John 14:15. "If you love me, you will keep my commandments." In other words, when we need a little help, we are to remember the way Jesus taught us to live. We are to love God and love our neighbor. We are to love even our enemies and do good to those who hate us. Rather than seek revenge when wronged, we are to forgive. Rather than justifying wrongful behavior, we need to ask to be forgiven. Make it a priority to act in the best interest of others. Be generous with your time, talent, and treasure. Feed the hungry. Do justice. Practice mercy. When you need a little help, do these things. Keep God's commandments.

More than a quarter century ago, Robert Fulghum wrote a book about the important lessons we learn in kindergarten. "Share everything. Play fair. Don't hit people. When you go out into the world, watch out for traffic, hold hands, and stick together."[2] Like the teachings of Jesus, these are good practices when you could use "a little help over here."

When seventeen-year-old Colleen ran out of gas two blocks from home, her father was concerned that she be reminded of another of Fulghum's lessons from kindergarten: "Clean up your own mess." In response to Colleen's cry for "a little help over here," Dad went to a hardware store and purchased a gas can. When he returned, he told his beloved daughter, "Before driving the car, always check the rearview mirror *and* check the gas gauge." Then he gifted her with that brand new gas can and told her to figure out how to get the stalled car home. "Clean up your own mess."

Colleen is now 45 years old. She has carried that same gas can in her car for the past 28 years and has never once had to use it. Colleen now has teenagers who are learning to drive. She tells them the story of the gas can and reminds them, "Before you drive the car, always check the rearview mirror *and* check the gas gauge."

Robert Fulghum's final lesson from kindergarten touched on a far more serious issue. He wrote, "Goldfish and hamsters and white mice and even the little seed in the Styrofoam cup (you planted in class) — they all die. So do we." I will die. You will die and every single person we love will die. And, quite simply, we have to learn to deal with that and a multitude of other painful realities.

157

That was the concern for Christine and Dan as they drove home from the doctor's office with the news that her cancer had returned with a vengeance. Assuaging the existential anxiety with which they dealt was going to require more than an admonition to keep the commandments. Dealing with the terror they experienced would even require more than a gentle reminder of the near presence of God. When they call out, "We need some help over here," they are talking about a fear that has the bitter taste of bile at the back of their throats; a fear that takes their breath away.

The apostles were dealing with a similar depth of anxiety on the night of the last supper. Jesus responded to their call for help with the promise of "the Advocate." This was nothing less than the Holy Spirit, the living presence of God, the power of the resurrected Christ in our midst. Jesus went on to say that this Advocate from God "will teach you everything, and remind you of all that I have said" (v. 26).

More than that, the power of the Holy Spirit will bring you peace. Not the peace that is declared by the standards of the world, but the peace that is the Shalom of God. As Jesus put it, "Peace I leave with you; my peace I give to you... Do not let your hearts be troubled, and do not let them be afraid."

God's response to our cry "can I get a little help over here" is the Advocate, the coming of the Holy Spirit, the bearer of the peace of God. God's Shalom quiets our fears and gives us the strength to deal with whatever the problem. God's Shalom offers courage to live triumphantly not only when faced by the first day of school or an empty gas tank, but to live courageously in the face of hurricanes, earthquakes, weapons of mass destruction, bombs planted at the finish line of the marathon, uncertain personal finances, divorce, grief at the loss of a loved one, our own terminal illness, as well as the courage to face and not fear all those other goulies and ghosties and long-leggedy beasties and things that go bump in the night.

You will have those moments similar to that young man pinned on the exercise bench with far too much weight pressing down on his chest. You will have those moments when you cry out, "Hey God, I need some help over here."

When that happens open your mind and your heart to the promise of faith. "Do not let your hearts be troubled, and do not let them be afraid."

Thanks be to God. Amen and amen.

---

1. Mary Hinkle Shore, "Commentary on John 14:23-29," www.theworkingpreacher.org, May 9, 2010.

2. Robert Fulghum, *All I Really Need to Know I Learned in Kindergarten* (released by several different publishers, first published in 1988).

Ascension of Our Lord
Luke 24:44-53

Then he said to them, "These are my words that I spoke to you while I was still with you — that everything written about me in the law of Moses, the prophets, and the psalms must be fulfilled." Then he opened their minds to understand the scriptures, and he said to them, "Thus it is written, that the Messiah is to suffer and to rise from the dead on the third day, and that repentance and forgiveness of sins is to be proclaimed in his name to all nations, beginning from Jerusalem. You are witnesses of these things. And see, I am sending upon you what my Father promised; so stay here in the city until you have been clothed with power from on high." Then he led them out as far as Bethany, and, lifting up his hands, he blessed them. While he was blessing them, he withdrew from them and was carried up into heaven. And they worshiped him, and returned to Jerusalem with great joy; and they were continually in the temple blessing God.

ASCENSION OF OUR LORD
LUKE 24:44-53

THE ASCENSION DAY
EXPERIENCE

The official ecclesiastical designation for this day is "The Feast of the Ascension." In keeping with its name, it commemorates the day the risen Christ ascended into heaven. Saint Augustine contended this holy day was first observed in the apostolic era. That would make it one of the earliest Christian holidays. By tradition, the date was established as the 39 days after Easter. That means it should always fall on a Thursday.

In many European nations, Ascension Thursday is widely celebrated as both a religious and a public holiday. It is religious in that the churches are open for a special time of worship. It is public in that Ascension Thursday is listed on national event calendars and government offices are closed. For that matter, banks and libraries are closed. There is no Ascension Thursday mail delivery and public transportation is likely to operate on a weekend schedule. On Ascension Day it is still possible to go to the hospital, report a fire, or call the police, but most workers have the day off.

Each European nation has its own way to observe the holiday. For instance, in France, people attend church in the morning and then they spend the rest of the day with their families, often outside enjoying the spring weather. In Portugal, in addition to attending church and spending time with family, the custom is to make wreaths of wheat, daisies, and olive branches. The wheat is said to symbolize an abundant harvest; the olives, a symbol of peace; the daisies are said to represent prosperity. They say that if you hang the wreath in your home, you can anticipate a year of peace, prosperity, and an abundant harvest.

Around Devonshire, England, there lingers an ancient superstition that any egg laid on Ascension Day will never go bad. It is supposed to be good luck to put an Ascension Day egg on the roof of your house. In Sweden, men gather in the woods as early as 3:00 or 4:00 a.m. in order to hear birds singing at sunrise. For people whose metabolism spikes late in the evening, wandering around in the woods before dawn has minimal appeal. However, for those who call themselves "morning people," just being in the forest when the sun comes up drips with possibilities of religious epiphany.

For many, Ascension Thursday offers an opportunity for worship with ample time for rest and relaxation with family and friends. Many Europeans enjoy the holiday so much that they take Friday as a personal day and make it a four-day weekend.

Obviously, that does not describe celebrating the Feast of the Ascension in the United States. Our local, state, and national governments do not declare it a public holiday. Our government agencies are open. Banks, courts, retail stores, manufacturing plants, and business offices run on a normal schedule. The restaurants not only continue to serve, I have never even heard of a restaurant having an "Ascension Day Special" on the menu.

It is even difficult to make a case that Ascension Thursday is a major celebration in the churches of the United States. In fact, many American churches don't even announce, let alone observe, the Feast of the Ascension. Even the American Roman Catholic church, which for centuries faithfully observed Ascension Thursday, has moved the observance to a Sunday — I assume in order to ensure better attendance.

A few years ago, I had the opportunity to experience the difference between a full-throttled European celebration of Ascension Thursday and the low-key American observance. My wife's sister, her husband, my wife, and I were traveling in Europe. We had planned the two-week trip to Germany, Denmark, Holland, and Switzerland with great care. Someone in our families had emigrated from one or more of these countries and we were going to get in touch with our roots. We had train tickets to get from country to country, rental cars reserved for touring within countries, and a long list of hotels where we had reservations. The itinerary had taken a year to complete and it was planned with the same attention to detail the Allies gave to the invasion on D-Day.

Everything went smoothly until the last stop on the trip — the 700-year-old city of Laufen, Switzerland, population 5,000. I had chosen this destination because my family had emigrated from this area nearly 150 years ago. This was to be a once-in-a-lifetime opportunity to learn about the origin of my rare and odd family name.

Early on a Wednesday evening we entered through a city gate in what remained of a medieval wall. We parked on the town square. Directly across from our car was a flower shop with my family name. I was thrilled. For the first time in my life I was going to have the opportunity to meet a stranger with my last name.

Then we checked into the hotel and learned that we had arrived on the evening of the four-day national holiday called Ascension. We were told the city had already begun to empty. By Thursday morning, all government offices would be closed. Most businesses, including most restaurants and the flower shop with my family name, would not be open.

The people at the hotel assured us that everything would be open for business as usual on Monday. Unfortunately we had to be in Zurich on Monday to catch a plane back to the

United States. I was not going to be able to research the government records of family members. I was not going to be able to go to the flower shop with my family name on the front window. The store's owner would be with family. After all, it was a national holiday.

We felt like first-time European visitors traveling to the United States the last week of November discovering that to be our four-day Thanksgiving weekend. Most things are closed and most people are with their families. On the one hand, it was not a matter of life or death. On the other hand, it was disappointing. A great distance had been traveled. Considerable time and money had been invested in this trip. In all likelihood we would never return to Laufen. Carefully laid plans had failed. New ones had to be made. It was inconvenient. It was disruptive. It was disappointing.

Since then, I have come to understand this introduction to a Swiss Ascension holiday as a means for understanding the biblical account of ascension. The apostles and other followers of Jesus had been devastated by his crucifixion. Three days later, however, their concerns were assuaged by the good news: "He has risen from the dead, hallelujah." In the ensuing days and even weeks they became accustomed to having Jesus nearby. The resurrected Christ was right there to answer their questions, to reassure them, and to quiet their fears.

Because human nature does not change from generation to generation, it seems logical the apostles and other followers of Jesus would have assumed he was going to remain with them, at least for the time being, perhaps for years to come.

About seven weeks after the resurrection, Jesus took his followers to the top of a high hill in the village of Bethany, not far from Jerusalem. Jesus turned toward them, lifted up his hands, and prayed for them. The gospel of Luke then says, "While he was blessing them, he withdrew from them and was carried up into heaven" (v. 51).

For a moment, consider the impact Jesus' ascension had on his followers. In the blink of an eye, Jesus was gone and they were left with only a warm breeze blowing across the hilltop. Keep in mind these followers already knew what it was like to lose Jesus. They had been there on the day of his crucifixion. They had felt their self-confidence drain from their lives and leach into the soil around them. They knew what it was like to be overwhelmed by a sense of aloneness and an uncertainty about the future. At the ascension, the feelings they had at the crucifixion must have returned. "Oh no, Jesus is gone again. What are we going to do now? How will we get along without him?"

That, my friends, is the experience of ascension. Most of us know what that is like. We have been there. It is felt when you were six years old and your best friend moved to another city. It is felt when you were sixteen and the first person for whom you had romantic feelings told you to get lost.

The experience of ascension can be much more serious. It is what happens when you are 35, married, and find a note on the refrigerator door. "I am leaving. I no longer love you. My attorney will be in touch. I plan to fight for sole custody of the children." It is the fear and uncertainty you feel for self and family when the company where you work closes and your job vanishes.

The Bible not only portrays these times often, it gives us guidance on how to proceed. In the First Testament, we are told that Uzziah was only sixteen years old when he became King of Judah. He remained on the throne for an incredibly long 52 years. In 2 Chronicles 26, we read details of the many accomplishments of Uzziah. For decades the nation benefited from having a king who served more than a generation. As frequently happens when powerful people serve long periods of time, the reign of Uzziah did not end well. Even with that caveat, Uzziah's death sent shock waves of grief and uncertainty across the country. Many had never known another king. There was a near universal lament, "Oh no, how will be get along without Uzziah?" The king's death launched a tidal wave of ascension experience.

In the midst of those hurting times, a prophet of God reassured the people with a vision. "In the year that King Uzziah died, I saw the Lord sitting on a throne, high and lofty; and the hem of his robe filled the temple" (Isaiah 6:1). To paraphrase the idea: when aloneness and uncertainty overwhelm, remember that God is close by.

The New Testament offers the same assurances for the ascension experience. In the first chapter of Acts, Luke tells us that before Jesus ascended into heaven he assured his followers that he was not abandoning them. The power of the Holy Spirit would come soon upon them. This power of God's holy presence would sustain them.

That is the same message of reassurance we hear in the hymn, "I Was There To Hear Your Borning Cry."[1] God goes with us through every event and every transition of our lives. When you find that you have wandered into an Ascension Day, fear not for God is near. Amen.

------

1. John Ylvisaker, "I Was There To Hear Your Borning Cry," 1985.

Easter 7
John 17:20-26

I ask not only on behalf of these, but also on behalf of those who will believe in me through their word, that they may all be one. As you, Father, are in me and I am in you, may they also be in us, so that the world may believe that you have sent me. The glory that you have given me I have given them, so that they may be one, as we are one, I in them and you in me, that they may become completely one, so that the world may know that you have sent me and have loved them even as you have loved me. Father, I desire that those also, whom you have given me, may be with me where I am, to see my glory, which you have given me because you loved me before the foundation of the world. Righteous Father, the world does not know you, but I know you; and these know that you have sent me. I made your name known to them, and I will make it known, so that the love with which you have loved me may be in them, and I in them.

LIVING BETWEEN
THE TIMES

On the church's calendar, today is called the "Seventh Sunday of Easter." Actually it is not a particularly familiar holy day. It is simply the Sunday that comes between the Ascension of our Lord and Pentecost, the birthday of Christ's church.

In other words, today is one of those "between the times Sunday." It falls between Jesus leaving his followers by ascending into heaven and the coming of the Holy Spirit. Rather than rendering the day insignificant, I think that is what makes it stand out. Today is a "between the times" Sunday and we are a "between the times" people. By that I mean we live between hearing the announcement of the angels, "Peace on earth and good will to all" and actually experiencing that Shalom of God. We live between praying "your kingdom come" and actually realizing "your will be done on earth as it is in heaven" (Matthew 6:10).

Today's lectionary gospel reading underscores our "between the times" status. In chapter 17 of John's gospel, our Lord offered the beautiful and powerful prayer for the unity of his followers. In verse 21 the master got to the heart of the issue when he prayed that all who follow him may be as one. "As you, Father, are in me and I am in you, may they also be in us, so that the world may believe that you have sent me."

Notice that demonstrating the oneness of the followers of Christ is to be our way of showing the world that Jesus is

Lord. Obviously, the church of Jesus Christ has fallen significantly short of realizing Jesus' unity prayer. When we drive the streets of any community we can see how differences of race, national origin, history, creeds, politics, personal opinion, and styles of worship have splintered Christ's universal church.

My practice in lectionary preaching is to search the internet to see how others handle the topic of the week. It came as no particular surprise that many ministers preaching on Jesus' prayer for the unity of all believers included lists of those they thought needed to be excluded for various reasons. At least some Christians do not set a priority to overcome our differences and live in unity with peace, justice, and harmony. Perhaps when they say "let us agree to disagree," they mean "let us agree to disagree until the Lord shows you that I am right."

Yet what happens in the church simply reflects what goes on in wider society. In 1776, we were just getting our act together as a nation. Among other things we needed an official seal with an official motto. A committee recommended what we know today as the "The Great Seal of the United States." It is a bald eagle with a fluttering yellow ribbon in its beak. On the ribbon is our motto in capital letters: *E PLURIBUS UNUM* — "Out of many, one." Originally, that motto was intended to express how the thirteen distinct colonies were coming together to form one nation. Over the years, we have started to broaden that understanding to include how we are one nation that has been formed by people who came from many places, who are of many races, who speak many languages, who practice many religions. We are *E PLURIBUS UNUM* — Out of many, we are one.

The 250th anniversary of adopting that motto is in the not-too-distant future. It seems a good time to assess, "How are we doing at being faithful to our national motto?" At the very least, I think we can agree that we have significant room for improvement. Some social commentators are even saying our national differences are about as entrenched and vitriolic as they were during the Civil War. In fact, when the political map of the United States is portrayed in red states and blue states, with few differences, it resembles the political divide of 1860.

Jesus prayed that we be one, but we are a divided church, a divided nation, and a divided world. And there seems to be a paucity of willingness to work toward unity — in the church, the nation, and the world.

A minister friend said he once heard the goal of our national motto *E PLURIBUS UNUM* trashed thoroughly, simply, and succinctly. This friend claimed that during a picnic table conversation at a family reunion, the topic meandered into how our nation is increasingly diverse. One of the participants remarked that he was thoroughly opposed to this trend. "Frankly," this cousin remarked, "I am not interested in diversity. I want to associate only with people who look like me, think like me, and believe like me."

When I asked the obvious question, my colleague in ministry confirmed that this cousin has trouble with relationships. New friends become former friends as soon as he discovers they have some differing political opinion or religious view, disagree with him about some current social issue, or don't meet his standards on how to conduct personal finances, raise children, or care for the lawn. This cousin did not even do well with family. He had been married four times and was estranged from all his grown children. That is not surprising. There is a high price for limiting associations to those who look like you, think like you, believe like you, and agree with you in every way and every topic. There are very few of those people in the world that can meet that standard. In fact, there may not be any.

Deep into his poem, *The Star Splitter*, Robert Frost put it this way:

If one by one we counted people out
For the least sin, it wouldn't take long
To get so we had no one left to live with.
For to be social is to be forgiving.
(public domain)

Each of us is unique. That is an underlying reality of God's created order. There is no one else in the world just like you or just like me. The billions of genes in the DNA of identical twins match — with only the tiniest differences. Yet identical twins will tell you they differ in a multitude of ways. We have to learn to live lovingly in human community with our differences because it is not possible to live with people just like us. As Robert Frost puts it, "to be social is to be forgiving."

The rub, of course, is that coming to terms with our differences and living in unity does not come naturally. It is hard work. Just getting along with folks who are almost like us takes enormous effort. Even the thought of living in unity with those who significantly differ from us can be overwhelming.

It might even be argued that there is good reason to resist welcoming differences. Our ancestors learned it was dangerous to trust those outside your own family. They knew from long experience that the family who lived on the other side of the mountain often did not have their best interest at heart. For hundreds of years, ideas about living in unity, peace, and harmony did not seem practical. In fact, collective human experience tends to confirm the views of that cousin at the family reunion picnic table. Because it is easiest, it must be best to associate only with people who look like us and think like us. We might even claim it is human nature to want to exclude those who differ so that we can associate with those who are most like us.

One of my favorite movies is the 1952 classic, *The African Queen*. The film takes place in Central Africa during the First World War. It stars Humphrey Bogart as Charlie Ulnut, a gin-swilling riverboat captain and Katherine Hepburn as Rose Sayer, a very straight-laced missionary. One night, as they float down a crocodile infested African river, Charlie gets rip-roaring drunk. Rose is aghast by his behavior and angrily scolds him. Charlie tries to justify his behavior by claiming getting drunk every once in a while is only human nature. Rose straightens her shoulders and says, "(Human) Nature, Mr. Ulnut, is what we are put on this earth to rise above."[1]

There is great truth in that observation. Wanting to associate only with people who are as much like us as humanly possible comes naturally. It is human nature. As people of faith, however, we are to live by a higher standard than doing what comes naturally. We are called to be the instruments of God in building a world where all the children of the Creator live in a unity of peace, harmony, and justice. That requires rising above human nature.

While it is a challenging task, it is possible to go against what comes naturally. As Paul puts it in the book of Romans, "Do not be conformed to this world, but be transformed by the renewing of your minds…" (Romans 12:2a). The New Living Translation, which makes an effort to translate the meaning of the text rather than simply translate the words, puts this passage beautifully. "Don't copy the behavior and customs of this world, but let God transform you into a new person by changing the way you think" (Romans 12:2a NLT).

Perhaps with a tinge of light-hearted humor, religion writer, Paul Prather suggested that there is a scientific basis for understanding the biblical admonition to be transformed by changing the way we think. Prather cited the science of neuroplasticity, also called brain plasticity or brain malleability. As close as I am able to understand the science, as human beings we are born with brains already downloaded with certain software. By that I mean, we come programmed with certain tendencies, predispositions, or personality traits. For instance, we think it is human nature to want to associate with people we consider just like us because our brain came programmed for that conclusion.

Fortunately, we are not doomed to live out our lives with the "software" with which we came. The computer that sits on top our shoulders is always getting updates and fixes for glitches based on differing needs and new experiences. To take that out of the language of computers and put it into the language of psychology, we have the capacity to learn, to mature, and to change. To put it into theological language of Romans 12:2, you do not have to copy the behavior and customs of the world, God can transform you into a new person by the renewal of your mind. That means God can make you into a new person by changing the way you think, by the way you believe, and by the way you behave.

To be perfectly honest, I do not know enough about the science of neuroplasticity or brain malleability to offer an informed opinion. I do know from experience and observation, however, that people can rise above what comes naturally to do what is right in the eyes of God.

Consider the story of Nelson Mandela, the first president of a united South Africa.[2] Mr. Mandela was born in a tiny village of cows, corn, and mud huts in Transkei, a region where black Africans were forced to live apart from white Africans. As a young man he gravitated toward violent groups that challenged the laws of apartheid. The white South African judicial system sentenced him to life in prison. For many of his nearly three decades in prison, he labored under a hot African sun using a hammer to make big rocks into little rocks. Indignity upon indignity was heaped upon him — including being denied permission to attend the funerals of his mother and his eldest son.

When Mr. Mandela was released from prison, he had reason to be angry and bitter about the way white South Africans had treated him. He had reason to say the time of white dominance was over; now it was time for black dominance. That did not happen. Instead of leading a bloody race war by calling for revenge of all past injustice, Nelson Mandela called for compromise, forgiveness, and reconciliation in a nation where all races are represented.

How does that happen? I submit to you it is just one of those mysteries of God's grace. It is a fulfillment of the promise that a person can be transformed by the renewal of the mind. For those of us who live between the times, it is an incomplete glimpse into how the world will look when the will of God is done on earth as it is in heaven. Amen and amen.

---

1. *The African Queen*, adapted from 1935 book of the same name by C.S. Forester; screen play by James Agee, released February 20, 1952.

2. Taken from an article by Bill Keller, *South Africa's Conqueror of Apartheid as Fighter, Prisoner, President and Symbol, The New York Times*, Friday, December 6, 2013, Section A, pp. 1, 16-18.

www.ingramcontent.com/pod-product-compliance
Lightning Source LLC
Chambersburg PA
CBHW052045090426
42739CB00010B/2054